ADVANCE PRAISE
LAUNCHING YOUR KID...

Few things are more worthy than setting up your children with a solid basis for life. By using a space mission analogy, Bob and Cheryl show us how we can "launch" our children safely and successfully into the world. The proven principles from Mission Control can be adapted to the raising of our children, setting them on a proper course for their lives. So get ready to launch! 5, 4, 3, 2, 1, lift off to a richly rewarding, life-changing reading experience.

—Dave Leestma, Former NASA astronaut

The Bible says that wise and godly children are a joy to their parents. I know that feeling for myself through my own grown kids. The church needs this book more than ever today! My prayer for readers is that you "launch your kids" in the same way Bob and Cheryl did!

—Dr. Gary Smalley, author of *The DNA of Relationships*

My friends Cheryl and Bob Reccord have amazed me again! They've written a book for parents that's full of great insight and practical ideas. It will motivate you to try simple suggestions that lead to big results. Your kids will discover their life's mission, your family will become their training ground, you and your spouse will become closer, and your family will have a blast together living the *on mission* lifestyle.

—Vonette Bright, Campus Crusade for Christ

Getting your children to adulthood healthy and emotionally stable is not enough. They need a spiritual mission that gives purpose to their lives. *Launching Your Kids for Life* gives a road map for parents who want their children to count in the kingdom of God.

—Gary D. Chapman, PhD, best-selling author of *The Five Love Languages*

As the parents of a five-year-old girl and a two-year-old boy, my husband and I have begun to look into the future, wondering how to give these precious little ones the right foundation not only to know the Lord for themselves, but to be salt and light to those around them. The school years will go by so quickly, and I've been praying for guidance to make the most of them. Bob and Cheryl Reccord's book has become one delightful answer to that prayer.

—Shaunti Feldhahn, author of *For Women Only*

As parents, our ultimate desire is to send our kids confidently into adulthood. Bob and Cheryl Reccord give us powerful, biblically-based tools to help us prepare our children for life. Their practical principles and value-based wisdom are an encouragment to every parent.

—Karol Ladd, best-selling author of *The Power of a Positive Mom*

Launching Your Kids for Life is innovative and encouraging. Thanks to Bob and Cheryl for showing us that what we can do for our children now will make a difference in their adult lives. It's all about preparation, and this book will teach you how to equip and encourage your children for life.

—Josh D. McDowell, author and speaker

The most important thing about reading this book is that your children will someday thank you for having read it! I highly recommend it to everyone who touches the life of a child.

—Billie Hanks Jr., founder and president
of International Evangelism Association and author

The real question for parents is not when will your children leave home, but how prepared will they be when they leave home. This insightful book will not only give them roots, but also give them wings!

—June Hunt, founder of the radio program *Hope for the Heart*

Launching Your Kids for Life is a must for parents or parents-to-be who desire to launch their kids into a full life of service and living for the Lord. Bob and Cheryl provide a Bible-based foundation and ample examples to choose from. Relating the launching of kids for life to the launching of astronauts on a mission in space makes it easy to understand and fun to read.

—Tom W. Holloway, retired NASA Shuttle Flight Director,
Shuttle Program Manager, and International Space Station Manager

LAUNCHING
YOUR
KIDS
FOR LIFE

BOB AND CHERYL
RECCORD

W PUBLISHING GROUP
A Division of Thomas Nelson Publishers
Since 1798

www.wpublishinggroup.com

Published by W Publishing Group, a Division of Thomas Nelson, Inc., P.O. Box 141000, Nashville, Tennessee 37214.

W Publishing Group books may be purchased in bulk for educational, business, fundraising, or sales promotional use. For information, please e-mail SpecialMarkets @ThomasNelson.com.

Unless otherwise indicated, Scripture quotations used in this book are from The Holy Bible, New International Version (NIV). Copyright ©1973, 1978, 1984, International Bible Society. Used by permission of Zondervan Bible Publishers.

Other Scripture references are from the following sources: The Message (MSG), copyright ©2002. Used by permission of NavPress Publishing Group. The New King James Version (NKJV®). Copyright © 1979, 1980, 1982 by Thomas Nelson, Inc. Used by permission. All rights reserved. The *Holy Bible,* New Living Translation (NLT), copyright © 1996. Used by permission of Tyndale House Publishers, Inc., Wheaton, IL 60189. All rights reserved.

Library of Congress Cataloging-in-Publication Data

Reccord, Robert E.
    Launching your kids for life / by Bob and Cheryl Reccord.
        p. cm.
    ISBN 0-8499-4549-6
    1. Parenting—Religious aspects—Christianity. 2. Child rearing—Religious aspects—Christianity. I. Reccord, Cheryl. II. Title.
    BV4526.3.R43 2005
    248.8'45—dc22

                                                            2004029449

Printed in the United States of America

05 06 07 08 RRD 9 8 7 6 5 4 3 2

To Christy Joy, our princess. Your overcoming tenacity has inspired us to never quit and shown us how to attack life with abandon.

To Bryan, our rock. Your quick wit and steadying influence have taught us to laugh at ourselves and enjoy the journey.

To Ashley, our peanut. Your passion for people and your caring heart for the underdog has reminded us of God's grace and helped us to keep our priorities straight.

CONTENTS

Acknowledgments

We learned from the astronauts who so generously gave of their time and expertise that the most critical point of a space shuttle mission is ignition. If everyone in Mission Control and the ground crew has done his or her job right, the shuttle launches in a blaze of glory.

It's the same with a book. Our indispensable ground crew included Helen Spore, who transcribed hours of dictation, and Carolyn Curtis, who shaped and forged our words and ideas into the laser-focused manuscript that became this book. Our friends at W Publishing Group—David Moberg, Laura Kendall, and their teams—partnered with us to make this a successful venture and a great read for parents who want to give their kids wings to fly.

Also, we were fortunate to include in our crew a capable team of experts: real-life moms and dads who have flown—and continue to fly—that mission called parenting. Their candor and graciousness in allowing us to tell their stories in fascinating detail are what take this book into what we think is a new stratosphere of help for parents hungry for answers, insights, and ideas to put into practice *today*. They include Beth and Steve Puckett, Debi and David Doverspike, Victoria Overton, Beverly Terrell, Carol and Randy Pope, Cindy and Carlos Ferrer, Mary and Ron Jenson, Pam and Mike Stabile, Tracey and Mike Parrott, Rhonda and Randy Singer, Diane and Jay Strack, Jeanine and Chuck Allen, Linda and Mike Ebert, Mels Carbonell, Doug Gilgrease, Allan Taylor, Claude Thomas, Julie Taylor, Dawn and Bryan Smith, and Betsy Batchelor. We love you guys!

FOREWORD

Children. They indeed are a gift. They challenge us, mystify us, sanctify us. They help us grow up. And they need our help as they grow up. We find it instructive that children are referred to in the Psalms as "arrows in the hands of a warrior" (127:4). Arrows were never meant to stay in the quiver; they were crafted for flight. They were designed for a mission—to be launched toward a target. And any archer worth his bowstring can tell you that training is what is needed if you are going to hit that target.

Do you feel the need to know how to become an effective parent who knows how to launch your child? Do you know what the right target is as you think about the day that you'll release your child? Have you ever wanted to be mentored by a couple who'd tell it like it really is?

If you're looking for practical training in knowing how to take aim, give your child a mission, and let go of your child, then you've found it. You are about to be trained by a pair of exceptionally gifted warriors who have learned their skills on the battlefield of parenting.

This book is more than good. It's stimulating. It's effective. It's a no-nonsense approach to a subject that has needed a book of this caliber. We wish we had read it before we launched our six arrows at the target. You're going to benefit immeasurably from the Reccords' seasoned counsel. These pages will help you recalibrate, correct, and better prepare for the day when you let them go.

Bob and Cheryl share hope and encouragement as they welcome you into the interior of their lives. And although they come from dramatically different backgrounds, together they have forged a plan for successfully launching their children with the ultimate mission. They remind us that nothing can be more important than equipping our children to transition into adulthood with their own faith and walk with Christ.

Bob and Cheryl Reccord are the real deal. No pretense or veneer. We like them. They are the kind of godly counselors who must surround us as we take on the challenge of raising a godly family in this culture. We trust them because they base the teachings of this book on the unchanging truth of Scripture and because they aren't afraid to admit their failures.

As you begin to read this book, we have one piece of encouragement: get a pen and a notebook for jotting down your thoughts, practical applications, and ideas that you don't want to forget. This book will give you the plan you've been looking for to let that arrow of yours fly.

Barbara and Dennis Rainey
Cofounders of FamilyLife

INTRODUCTION

Frankly, this is a book we wish had been available when our kids were small.

No, it's not that we were and are such perfect parents. In fact, our beginning was pretty modest. You'll see what we mean.

We as coauthors (Bob and Cheryl) worked hard to write a book that will interest *both* mothers and fathers, but this introduction has some stories best told from Cheryl's point of view . . .

When I was seven months pregnant with Christy, our oldest, I called a friend who'd recently had a baby to ask if she could teach me to change a diaper and give a bottle. She invited me over. After observing my clumsy attempts to pin on a diaper (yes, we are old enough to have actually used cloth diapers!), she said, "I thought you had to be kidding me about not knowing how to do this! But I can see that you really *don't* know!" To make matters worse, Bob had never even *held* a baby until a nurse placed Christy in his arms as we left the hospital. I guess the best way to describe us is that we were dumber than dirt!

But with the confidence that comes with youth and ignorance, we headed home with our precious baby girl, absolutely certain we would be great parents. *What could possibly be so hard about raising kids?* we figured. *Hey, didn't we turn out okay?*

Our buoyant self-assurance lasted . . . all of four days.

It was during one of those interminable sleepless nights with a colicky baby when Bob turned to me and lovingly asked, "Explain to me one more time why we looked forward to this for nine months?"

If only we'd known then what we know now. We needed this book! Not to help us get our baby back to sleep that night. But to help us see God's plan for her and—more important to us as parents—to show us the process we would guide her through as she discovered that plan.

So now that we're older and wiser, we've written the book we think other parents like us need. Parents who want their children to know God and recognize His calling in their lives. Parents who long to launch their kids successfully. Parents who want to serve Him and show their kids how to do the same with intentionality (what we call being *on mission*). Parents who need some encouragement and advice and, most of all, some solid, applicable ideas.

If only we'd done then what we've done now, life might have been simpler. You see, we've looked around and observed parents who have great relationships with their kids—and whose kids are excited about their walk with God—and we've spent time finding out how they accomplished it. Amazingly, while their stories are as different as their kids, we've found that the same basic principles are true in all of them. So this is not a book that tells you just *our* great ideas (though we do share some), but a book that focuses on the fun of discovering *God's* principles and how to enjoy living them out in the warp and woof of family life through the stories of families who've done it well.

Hmmm, you may wonder, *will this book pile on more guilt about what I'm not doing as a parent?* Absolutely not! We know that if you're parenting in the twenty-first century, you don't need anything else to drag you down or more tasks to pack into your schedule. In fact, what we're hoping to do is *lighten* your load by sharing with you how to weave a life of spiritual legacy with your kids through activities you're already doing. Then they'll be ready for the day when they fly from your nest, knowing beyond a shadow of a doubt that they've been made to count.

You may be thinking, *The time when they will leave is so far away.* We thought so too. Yet I vividly remember facing the fact that our job as parents is literally to work ourselves out of a job. When our son, Bryan, was two and a half, I took him to an open house to visit his preschool. I was certain he was anxious about this new experience, so I rehearsed in my mind all the reassuring words I could say to help him launch into school life. I found myself holding his hand, pulling him just a little closer to me so he would sense how secure he was. Well, we walked down the stairs and hadn't even arrived where the group was meeting when he looked up at me and said, "It's okay, Mommy; you can go now. I'm fine." Well, *he* might have been fine, but I wasn't! After all, he needed me close. Very close! But there he was, ready to turn loose and find his niche. How dare he?

Some things just don't change. Oh, I finally *did* let him go. I let him go off to school, and then to college (I didn't even move into the apartments across from his dorm, as I'd threatened). In fact, just recently, he moved off to his first real job. And even more recently, I *let* him get married! And it all happened in the blink of an eye.

You see, it really is inevitable. Our children actually do grow up and leave our nests. So the question is not *Will they leave home?* but *How prepared will they be when they leave home?*

We surveyed the landscape of books on parenting and found that most tell how to give our children *roots.* But we know another element crucial to the development of our children: giving them the blessing of *wings*. If we as parents miss this vital step, then as a family we'll be like the relay-race team that has record-winning sprinters who can't pass off the baton successfully. Sure, their times may be great, but they will lose the race.

We also found books dealing with fatherhood or motherhood but rarely both. So despite an introduction Cheryl mostly wrote (she's a homemaker whose empty-nest years are evolving into a career of writing, public speaking, and life coaching), you'll also find much in the book that appeals to men—or whoever in your marriage is process-oriented and logical and can appreciate how launching one of NASA's well-engineered spacecrafts is really a lot like launching your kids for life. Believe it or not, we'll put you on board a space shuttle launch and show what the crew does through countdown and beyond. We were fortunate to find several high-ranking NASA executives and astronauts to consult with who are just as excited about this metaphor as we are.

So if technology turns you on—or you just can't escape it (and who can these days?)—don't shy away from this book, thinking it's about cuddly babies, adorable youngsters, perfectly behaved teenagers, and—well, you get the idea. Parenting is hard. The people you'll meet are overcoming tough obstacles. They're real. And so are we.

Guess what else is real? The fact that in some marriages both partners aren't on board with what it takes to launch a Christ-following child. We'll deal with that too. In fact, Bob (whose background ranges from pastoring to business and industry to leading a missions agency) addresses this issue in a way we think will provide hope and encouragement for readers who are raising kids alone or without the support of a spouse fully committed to biblical principles. If that's you, take heart. We affirm you. Many ideas presented in these pages can be implemented one-on-one.

It's T minus twenty minutes, parents and grandparents. Please join us on the launching pad!

Part I

Ways to Prepare for a Successful Launch

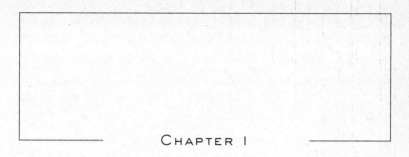

CHAPTER 1

IMAGINE

Imagine this: suddenly, you're not a reader of this book, but someone who's been *affected* by a reader of this book. In other words, you've met someone who bought this book—someone who got specific ideas for how to instill the value of living an *on mission* lifestyle into his or her kids. Here's what that experience might be like . . .

Since we're reinventing you anyway, let's say you don't follow Christ, but you're good friends with a family named the Pucketts. Maybe you live in their neighborhood, play a sport with a member of the family, or do business with Steve's firm. Maybe you know Beth from a club or one of their kids from Scouts or Little League.

You know they "go to church"—whatever that means—so when they invite you to one of their kids' baptisms, followed by lunch on their deck, you figure, *Why not go?* It would be rude not to; the Pucketts know your Sunday mornings are pretty much wide open.

Besides, it would be a great way to meet some new people. The Pucketts are nice; their friends might be nice too.

So you show up. You have a *general* idea what church is about—baby in a manger, man on a cross—but you're not sure what a "baptism" is or why it's such a big deal. So you take a seat and wait for the show to begin.

Funny thing, a show really *does* begin—pretty impressive production too. *Wow, when did they start putting all this video equipment in churches, anyway?* Up on a huge screen appears the Pucketts' son Mitchell. He's talking into the camera. It's like a documentary with bits of home movies spliced in. Some baby shots. There's Steve when his hair was a little less gray. Beth looking fit as always, though younger. *Hmmm.* Now Mitchell is older. Doing family stuff, school stuff, this and that. Now the scenes shift a bit, and you see some church activity. Seems as if church is more than Christmas and Easter for the Pucketts. Well, you knew as much. Then the camera goes back to Mitchell today. He looks just as you know him, yet he seems different somehow—more serious. As if what he's saying is more important than telling about his science project. It's coming from his gut. He's really into it.

He's talking about "knowing Christ," "making a commitment," "trusting the Lord." This makes you vaguely uncomfortable, yet you're intrigued . . . glued to the image, in fact, of this boy you've known, growing up in this family you've known, talking with such maturity about his faith!

Finally, they dunk him. You knew that was coming too, although you weren't sure just how they would accomplish it, this "baptism."

Suddenly, a mood that was quiet is joyous. You feel swept up by that happiness too. You know the boy has done something important, and you know the parents are proud and thrilled.

You go to the luncheon and chat up the friends. Nice baptism, nice church, yadda, yadda. "Wasn't his testimony wonderful?" someone asks you. *Testimony?* You're not sure how to respond. Oh, that video . . . sure, it was great, just great. You smile inwardly, imagining your friends' kid on a witness stand giving a testimony in a court of law. But come to think of it, that's not too far off, based on what the boy said about what he knows . . .

Suddenly the party changes. Beth shows up with some balloons, really colorful ones. She's making it into a game. "Who knows what the colors mean?" she asks. *Hmmm.* They're primary colors, some of them. *Okay, I get it: Jesus is Mitchell's primary man!* You start to make that guess when you realize how foolish it will sound if you're wrong. Besides, it's more of a kids' game. In fact, kids are giving answers, and Beth is nodding her head. Now Steve is beside her, getting into the act. This colored balloon thing is turning out to be a big deal too.

This Puckett family is incredible. They're talking about some very heavy stuff by using these colored balloons: God, man, sin, separation from God, Christ as a bridge. Wow! You're not sure you understand it all, but you're getting their drift. And you're getting another message—loud and clear. This Puckett family talks about God *out loud.* They talk about God as if He's a party guest, as if He's someone they know. And the *kids* talk about God like that, not just Beth and Steve. Oh, sure, they're kids, so they cut up a bit. But they talk about God and about talking *to* God . . . *well, like talking to me!*

Okay, Back to Reality, Reader

You're you, not this mythical guest at the Puckett family baptism and luncheon. But for a few paragraphs, you could almost relate to him or her, couldn't you? That's because the Pucketts, a real family we know and love, not only serve the Lord by telling others about Him but teach their kids to live their faith out loud too. They have made living an *on mission* lifestyle a priority teaching in their home.

In practice, what does this mean? It means they have intentionally and deliberately taught their kids to put God first and to demonstrate to others that this is how they live. They live to honor God, because He sent His Son to die for their sins. And, yes, they find ways to weave this into their day-to-day lives.

For example, Steve and Beth really did make a video for each child's baptism. That's well and good. It's a keepsake, and it helps to mark a rite of passage that all Christian parents hope their kids achieve. But how did they also make the experience specifically *on mission*? How did they model the behavior they hope their kids adopt when they grow up, settle down, and start families of their own?

They invited nonbelieving friends to the event. And then they punched it up a notch with the balloons. So instead of just colorful decorations, the balloons gave them an opportunity to explain the gospel using colors (black for sin, red for blood, etc.). In other words, when the Pucketts planned the event, they added some details to the checklist. In addition to where their guests would park and what food they would serve, the Pucketts thought, *What can we use to tell the gospel that fits in with a party atmosphere? And what people do we need to make sure are there so they can hear it?*

Voilà! Enter stage left our fictitious guest—or maybe not so fictitious after all, since the Pucketts make it a point to spend time with nonbelievers. And that's part of being *on mission* too. In fact, it's an essential part if you're going to reach people for Christ and teach your children to do the same.

Is that what you want to do? To have a family life so in tune with God that non-Christian friends and family can sense it, can experience it, can grow toward a relationship with Christ from it—without thinking you're loony? To raise children so comfortable with their faith they can articulate it to grumpy Uncle Harry, to your clueless friend from the office who comes over for coffee, or to the messed-up teenager next door? To launch kids who, after discovering God's missions for their lives, soar off confidently with wings of their own?

These are worthy goals for a parent. But to accomplish them, we believe you must make a special effort. Not necessarily a *difficult* effort, but an effort that you consider, plan, and put into action. And that's why we wrote this book: to give you specific ideas, such as the Pucketts' baptism party and one family's motto, "Go mad!" To give you a tool our family uses called *guidestones* to celebrate an important moment and make it even more meaningful with a plaque you personalize for your family (we'll share more about that later). To give you a biblical basis for your role and responsibility as a mom or dad. And to encourage you with advice from parents who have been in the trenches and pass along their wisdom with incredible candor.

For this journey, all you need is a willingness to get out of your safe, familiar bubble, to take a risk, a very *big* risk, leaving your comfort zone . . . maybe even the stratosphere!

TRIUMPH AND TRAGEDY

Many readers of this book may remember the 1980s—or may have heard about that decade. The space shuttle program was in high gear. It was a time of spectacular triumph, but also great tragedy.

And we needed some triumph. In the previous decade U.S. President Richard M. Nixon had resigned in disgrace. But he did have a vision and gave his executive approval for the development of the space shuttle. The shuttle program would be another historic milestone in exploring what one of Nixon's predecessors (President John F. Kennedy) called the New Frontier.

The space shuttle elevated our technology to an advanced level and captured our imaginations once again. For the first time in history, a primary spaceship would be used repeatedly to carry explorers into space and eventually dock with space stations. Wow!

From inception to liftoff, the development process took nine years. *Columbia* made its debut April 12, 1981. The spaceship looked like nothing we had ever seen before. It was a dart-shaped, sweptwing vehicle attached to an oversized exterior fuel tank and solid booster rockets. *Columbia's* first voyage lasted fifty-four hours, with no major hitches.

Between 1983 and 1985, three more sweptwing masterpieces joined the fleet: *Challenger, Discovery,* and *Atlantis.* Those were heady years for NASA. The close of 1985 brought the American space program to the point where more people had flown into space aboard the shuttle than on all previous spacecraft combined. Triumph!

But 1986 began with tragedy. On January 28, *Challenger* brought the first in-flight deaths of astronauts in the U.S. space program's history. Seven fearless astronauts lost their lives shortly after takeoff as a horrified world watched. The problem was a faulty O-ring on one of *Challenger's* twin solid rockets, a small engineering detail in a gigantic spaceship. The O-ring could not stand up to the extreme conditions of launch. As a result, hot gases burst through and ruptured seals and joints, leading to the catastrophic explosion and bringing a halt to the space shuttle program for thirty-two months. NASA and its congressional overseers grounded the remaining spaceships and their highly trained crews. It was time for a major correction.

IMAGINE YOU'RE AN ASTRONAUT

"Hey, I'm holding a book on parenting," you say, "so what does the space shuttle have to do with my kids?"

Again, we (Bob and Cheryl, parents of three) will show you how raising a child is much like NASA launching a spacecraft. To prepare we consulted with NASA astronauts and executives.

Meanwhile, fasten your safety belt, make sure you have a rich supply of oxygen available, and let's see what it takes to successfully launch and carry out a shuttle mission. You'll be amazed at the parallels you see with raising your kids!

First, imagine that *you* are an astronaut. In our analogy, the astronaut represents the child. And if you think this exhilarating description of a launch sounds like some of your own growing-up years, it should. You were a kid once too.

Your launch begins with an explosive upward thrust in which the shuttle moves from a dead stop on the launching pad to 17,500 miles per hour in 8.5 minutes. At launch minus two minutes and thirty seconds, your helmet visor swings down over your face, and your personal oxygen begins to flow. At launch minus ten seconds, you sense the rumbling rush of water from the deluge system far below the cockpit. At launch minus six seconds, the three main engines ignite, then throttle up and violently shake your entire orbiter assembly. When the solid rocket boosters kick in, the gravitational force on you *immediately* jumps all the way up to three Gs.

Before the main engines cut off and with the G-forces this strong, you feel as if a large animal is sitting on your chest. That's because of the enormous weight of three Gs of pressure. Then, at the moment of main engine cutoff, you *immediately* go from three Gs down to zero. Now that's drastic. As you're reading this book, you're experiencing one G due to the force exerted by Earth's gravity. But in space, astronauts are in free fall and experience no force due to gravity.

Okay, reader, take a breath. Were you *there*? Ready to burst free but being pulled back by incredible forces that finally let go, and now you seem to be in a complete free fall?

Maybe you didn't experience this in a space shuttle, but do you remember that ride called *growing up*? It was full of anticipation, exhilaration, and sometimes palm-sweating fear. Do you remember that first day of school, wanting the adventure but not quite ready to break out of your safe orbit at home? Your first piano recital? First time up to bat? How about the day your bike skidded out from under you, and you felt you were in a free fall all the way down to that rough and unforgiving pavement? Things got better when Mom and Dad showed up and gathered you and your beloved bike in their arms. But sometimes they were just close enough to cheer you on. *You* were the one who had to march up to that grand piano and strike the first chord of the sonata you had practiced so long. *You* were the one who had to step up to home plate with a bat you could barely swing and legs so rubbery you thought you might fall.

In the beginning of a space shuttle mission, the crew is strapped in tightly and operating under the protective control of Florida's Kennedy Space Center. Once the shuttle clears the launch tower, Flight Control switches to Mission Control at the Johnson Space Center in Houston. Teams there are working around the clock to assure the astronauts a safe and productive journey and to give advice on how the crew can best carry out its mission.

Here's where our analogy really gets interesting. While the astronauts are very dependent on Mission Control, they do have the authority to override Mission Control if they think a change is necessary. So ultimately the astronauts are responsible for their own missions.

This reminds us of the relationship of a child to his or her parents (Mission Control) and to other influencers (the ground crew of grandparents, pastors, coaches, teachers, and so on). They're all standing by, watching, ever ready with data, opinions, and advice. They desperately want the mission (the child's life) to be a success and will do everything they can to help during the launch and throughout the flight. By liftoff, will the astronaut remember all his training, all he's been taught? Will she tune in to Mission Control, accepting help from the ground crew? Will the mission be successful?

In Flight

A specific-colored patch or dot identifies each crew member's equipment. For example, the commander may be red, the pilot yellow, the flight engineer or mission specialists 1, 2, 3, and 4 might use blue, green, orange, and brown, and the payload specialist's color could be purple. Even their food, selected before flight, is color-coded so each member knows which meal is his or hers. (Sound a little like camp? Or reading groups at school? Wait, there's more.) Changes take place during the flight, such as astronauts actually growing taller due to the weightless environment and a lengthening of the spine. This "growth" can cause lower backaches. Their spacesuits must be sized to accommodate this growth, about one inch on average. (Who knew astronauts "grew" into their clothes?)

When you're speeding through orbit in a shuttle, you're moving at 17,500 miles per hour—nearly five miles per second!—and you're high enough to see the curve of the earth below. But there are side effects to such an exhilarating ride. (Remember climbing out of the tilt-a-whirl ride in the amusement park and stumbling back to your parents—laughing but holding your stomach?) The weightless environment aboard a spacecraft often causes nausea as the fluids within the body shift significantly. Due to weightlessness and fluid shifts in the head, astronauts can feel as if they have a bad cold, and their taste buds even change. Foods with pleasant, enjoyable tastes on Earth suddenly seem dull. In space astronauts prefer spicier food than they might order back home.

Spacewalks are a high point. That's when astronauts leave the orbiter to work outside their craft in outer space itself. Tethered to the moving spacecraft, they can exercise surprising freedom. The sense of movement is overwhelming as they watch Earth in the vast distance while hurtling at 18,000 miles per hour. Temperatures outside the orbiter are extreme: as low as -165 degrees Fahrenheit up to a toasty 200 degrees Fahrenheit, depending on whether the nose of the shuttle faces deep outer space or the sun. (In kid terms: Growing up can be cool—or things can heat up in a hurry, all in the blink of an eye.)

THINKING OUTSIDE THE BOX

Although Mission Control and the ground crew are available by satellite transmission, astronauts need to be creative, using what they've learned and can apply on their own.

NASA astronauts told us of times during shuttle missions when analyzing their problems with a fresh perspective, also called *thinking* (or *coloring*) *outside the box,* was absolutely essential to accomplishing the mission. On one flight, the shuttle crew tried to snag and repair a satellite, but with little success. Finally, they decided to send out three astronauts instead of two to grab the satellite. That's when Mission Control instructed the astronauts to go to bed, adding that the scientists and engineers in the ground crew would think about the idea overnight. Mission Control was concerned about both success and safety. Could three astronauts pass through the air lock? It sounded risky.

But during the night three astronauts attempted the maneuver in the training pool within their shuttle and concluded it could be done. The next day the crew was given the "Go" to use three astronauts to capture the satellite. Working together, attempting something that had never been done before, the three stopped the satellite from rotating and captured it. Think what would have happened to a multimillion-dollar piece of highly engineered scientific equipment had somebody not been willing to think outside the box.

Isn't that what we all want for our children—for them to accomplish their missions? For them to break out of their boundaries? For them to succeed?

As Christ-followers, we believe that success is discovering God's mission for our lives and then accomplishing it to the best of our ability. As Christian parents, we know our role is to provide direction from Mission Control and help from the ground crew. And no matter how much we try to prepare them for their mission, we know one day our children will fly on their own. When they do, we want them to experience triumph, not tragedy.

When we were preparing our three—Christy, Bryan, and Ashley— we were hungry to read a book like this. As we mentioned in the introduction, we needed much of the insight and advice we'll share with you based on our own family and the dozen or so other families you'll meet in this book. They're fascinating! All have experienced heartbreak and joy, tragedy and triumph, and like you, they expressed a longing to have a resource for parents who want to launch their kids successfully on the missions in life that God has planned for them.

But the responsibility of Mission Control can be overwhelming. So we've come up with a list of eight principles to apply to your parenting. We believe that if you teach these to your children in those first eighteen or so years they're at home in your care, they'll have the foundation on which to find and follow their lives' missions. Our principles are

1. God prepared a unique plan and calling for your life even before you were born.

2. God calls you to a life-changing relationship with Him through Jesus Christ.

3. God calls you to partner with Him in a mission that is bigger than you are.

4. God calls you to be *on mission* with Him right where you are—starting now.

5. God reveals His mission through His Word, His Spirit, wise counsel, and His work in circumstances around you.

6. God will repeatedly bring you to crossroads of choice as He forges you for His mission.

7. God guides you and provides for your mission one step at a time.

8. When you answer God's call, you will experience His pleasure and change your world.

You may have seen this list in Bob's previous book *Made to Count* (W Publishing Group, 2004, coauthored with Randy Singer). Our readers for that book are adults of all ages who want to discover what to do with their lives, who want to live lives of real significance.

But if you're holding this book, you're most likely a parent who wants to instill these principles into the hearts of your children. We'll flesh out the eight principles in more detail later.

For now, we'll conclude this chapter with one overarching lesson we've learned from all our research, introspection, and interviews: *a sense of humor is essential in raising a family.* (We'll talk more about this in chapter 24.) Kids who grow up in homes with lots of fun and laughter turn out better. We heard this over and over as we spoke to the families you'll meet. And we found it true in our own lives. It seems that a little levity is a great bonding element in relationships, especially in families who are trying to launch their children into adulthood according to God's plan for their lives.

In fact, we even heard about the value of humor from our NASA experts. They told us a story about a shuttle flight when the astronauts decided to have a little fun—even though, at first, Mission Control disapproved. The launch was scheduled for November. By the end of October, the astronauts were weary of the stress of preparation: the tests and simulations at the Kennedy Space Center that precede a launch. Word leaked out that they wanted to wear Halloween masks for one critical test. Mission Control made it clear that this sort of tomfoolery would not be acceptable, but the shuttle crew was not deterred. Okay, no masks, they agreed, realizing how childish the idea sounded. Yet they were desperate to do *something* to relieve the stress with some fun!

The solution came to them as they gazed at the bald head of one of their crew members, Story Musgrave. He also happened to be famous around KSC for wearing a distinctive style of sunglasses. Imagine the surprise and laughter on the day of their countdown test when the whole crew showed up with shaved heads and identical sunglasses!

Yes, a sense of humor is essential. In the next few chapters, you'll learn how important it is to parenting and to a healthy family life. And we hope this book provides you with some lighter moments as well as inspiration. As we mentioned earlier, the ideas are meant to lighten your load, not add a burdensome to-do list. Most require just a bit of attitude adjustment, a tweaking of your communication skills. You'll learn how to make simple changes in your parenting that will have lasting results in your children's futures.

Sometimes we'll recommend a solution that requires a bit more work on your part. For example, you'll discover our ideas for marking milestones—which we call *guidestones*—in your children's growth on their way to the launching pad. What's different about our book is that we'll also point you to the resources you'll need to create your guidestones in a way that honors your family's individuality, celebrates your child's identity, and personalizes your message.

After all, it's *your* family, Mom and Dad. You're Mission Control.

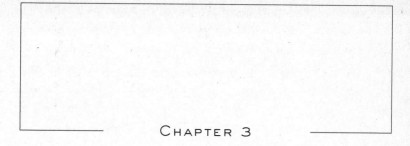

CHAPTER 3

NUGGETS OF WISDOM

A *home full of joy and laughter and fun.* We identified that as the number-one common denominator in healthy families. In our interviews we discovered that parents or couples who are trying to launch their kids *on mission* are serious about having a good time! The pursuit of happiness is one of the foundations of their marriage, and they commit early on to create a home and family environment that celebrate joy.

Laughter, rich and uproarious, punctuates their family's conversations. They have fun together. They seek joy. And their friends of all ages know it and are attracted to the warmth of their home. As a result, people notice and admire their lifestyle, which provides a great entrée to reaching nonbelievers. In fact, with just about everybody we interviewed, we practically had to stand in line. These folks are popular! People seek them out. Kids want to hang out at their houses. You'll read more about all this in the pages and chapters to come, including the story of one family, the Allens, who laugh even in the face of everyone's worst nightmare, cancer.

What other trends did we find? The advice we uncovered runs the gamut. Most is woven through the book, nuggets of wisdom you'll discover in the stories of families who have been in the trenches of parenting. But we'll unpack a few selected bits of wisdom in this chapter. Here's a summary to whet your appetite . . .

- Find a mentor.
- Be a parent, not your child's friend.
- Develop a structured method of praying for your child.
- Model good behavior for your children.
- Plug into a strong community of faith.

FIND A MENTOR

Several people we interviewed said they were influenced by mentors. And looking back on our days as young parents, we wish we'd picked a few people's brains ourselves. We could have benefited from the wisdom and experience of couples who were older than us.

Beverly Terrell is that kind of woman. And because we've identified her as a mentor, you probably think she and her (late) husband, Jack, were just about perfect parents, right? Well, not if you call having a son arrive home high as a kite on drugs to be the outcome of perfect parenting.

We promise to tell you Beverly's story, but first we need to make three points about mentoring.

First, if you as a parent don't have a mentor, we urge you to find one. Admit to yourself and to an older friend you admire that you could use some help. And then follow up by being vulnerable and asking your mentor to be vulnerable too. Parenting is not for wimps. Doing it well requires the courage to be real and teachable.

Second, some of the best mentors are folks whose parenting years were a big challenge. For one thing, they went through a lot, and if you're fortunate, they'll share with you their richest wisdom. Don't we all learn best through our mistakes and hardships? It's not necessary to pick someone as a mentor whose kids seem perfect.

Third, we want you to know that our high regard for mentoring is one of our motivations for writing this book. And that's why we'll introduce you to a number of parents who share their insights. They were kind enough to open up, and we're delighted to tell you what they had to say. We were humbled by their candor. And we pass along their ideas with huge respect for them as godly parents.

The Terrells would have been great choices for our mentors because of their strong communication skills; they cut right to the chase, never whitewashing the circumstances and instead seeing how God used the situation to teach and build. One story from their family's past is a great illustration. It's all the more dramatic in the retelling, because the Terrell kids turned out to be such godly adults. We think the open communication style of their parents is one reason.

Jack Jr. had been out watching the fireworks at Dallas's Cotton Bowl. He and his friends had dropped some LSD before they went. We'll let Beverly explain in her own words:

> Drug users will tell you there's nothing like the color of fireworks when you've had a few drugs. They enhance the colors—they're absolutely dazzling. Anyway, Jack Jr. knew he still had a curfew even though he was in college. He knew he had to be home by midnight. So they took the drugs before they went to the Cotton Bowl, returned to an apartment in North Dallas, and he was waiting until 11:30 for the drugs to wear off so he could head home. He knew his father and I always waited up for him, made sure he

got home all right. And I always checked his eyeballs to see if his pupils were dilated.

He and his friend Joy were both waiting it out, hoping the drugs would wear off so they could slip past their parents when they came home. For some reason Jack and Joy started talking to each other about Jesus, even though they were high. Jesus just came into their conversation. (That's why I know spiritual warfare prayers really pay off.)

So, first they're high on acid watching fireworks, and then they're talking about Jesus. But the thing is, neither of them could say His name. Jack remembered a Scripture we'd taught him about that [1 Cor. 12:3]—how you tell a false prophet from a real one is whether he can name the Savior. Jack said, "Do you know who that is?" Joy said, "I know who that is." He said, "Then say His name." And Joy couldn't say His name. She said, "Well, you say His name." And Jack couldn't either. They looked at each other and said, "Oh, my gosh, this is demonic."

The kids in the other room were starting to mainline heroin. Jack had always been afraid of needles, but he was considering doing it that night. (He told us later, looking back when he had a chance to process all this, that he could see how God had protected him.) He grabbed Joy by the hand and said, "Let's get out of here." They ran out of the apartment, giving no explanation to their friends. I've always believed that if the thought of Jesus hadn't stopped them, they would have mainlined, and he might have died that very night.

They came to our house. Jack and I were in bed. The lights were turned out, and they were silhouetted in the doorway of our bedroom. Jack Jr. said, "Mom and Dad, are you awake?" We said, "Yeah, we're waiting for you to come home." He said, "Well, we need help." We got out of bed and went into the living room, and for more than two hours we fought spiritual warfare with those kids.

The presence of the adversary was as real as any service I've ever been in where you feel that sweet Spirit of the Lord. I was having difficulty breathing. Jack and I just took turns sitting with them and quoting Scripture. Finally, Jack Jr. said, "Dad, I want to get out of this, and I want to walk away, but I can't leave my friends. I just can't be free of this."

That's when my husband said, "If the Son makes you free, you are free indeed. Now repeat that after me." Jack Jr. said, "If the Son makes me free, I am free indeed." He said it three times. Then he paused, and I'll never forget the look on my son's face. I mean, it was like a lamp had just flooded that living room with light. I thought I was going to hyperventilate. And Joy was kneeling at our sofa and had her head down. She said she felt the light as well, and she said, "Me too, Jesus. If you make me free, I'm free indeed." She repeated it three times. It was just like spiritual electricity, the Spirit of God telegraphing that to all four of us sitting in that room.

Our son claimed his freedom that night. (And later, all but two of that group of kids came to know the Lord in the next year or two.)

Well, the next Sunday after our night of spiritual warfare in the living room, Dr. Bill Nix, who taught for years at Dallas Theological Seminary, was our church's teacher in the college department. Jack Jr. had not changed his looks—he still had shoulder-length hair but always kept it clean—yet that Sunday his face was so different. As Bill told it, when Jack Jr. walked through the room full of college kids who were home for the summer, it was like the parting of the Red Sea. They stopped talking and just looked at him. Since he had claimed his freedom in the Lord, his countenance had become so different. The Spirit of God was so in control where the adversary had been so in control. Now he was a Christian. It was obvious just by looking at him. And yet we had not told anyone yet, and neither had he.

Maybe you can see why we wish we'd profited from Beverly's wisdom much sooner—not because drugs were a problem in our family (they were not), but because she understands good and evil and has seen both up close. That's an incredible experience. And we could have learned a lot from hearing how she and her husband, Jack, had raised their children with Bible study and morning devotions around the breakfast table, and yet Jack Jr. had still gone through this frightening circumstance. So had his friends, yet most of them were church kids. What gives parents this kind of strength—the love, the patience, the rock-solid grace to stand by their kids even while they are misbehaving and breaking their hearts?

For one thing, in the case of the Terrells, they had seen a miracle of God in their own family. They had asked God to change their metabolism! That's right. Beverly and Jack were night owls, and they asked God to change them to become morning people, because they realized they needed to have quality devotional times with their children over the breakfast table, and they could not accomplish that unless they drastically changed their routine.

Explains Beverly, "We began to make it a matter of prayer for God to change Jack and me as parents into early people. We believe in the quickening power of the Holy Spirit, not just to quicken our spirits but to quicken our bodies as well. We saw Him do that in just a matter of months."

Her best advice: parents should be united in their goal. "Know that you are custodians of these children for just a few years. They're just on loan to you. You have to teach them obedience and respect for you, so they will honor their heavenly Father as adults. It's the best gift you can give them."

BE A PARENT, NOT YOUR CHILD'S FRIEND

Here's our simple advice on this: don't compromise the role God assigned to you. Your child needs you to be a parent, not just a friend. A lot of our interviewees felt the same way. Listen to the wisdom of one of our friends.

Allan Taylor said:

I hear so many parents say, "I just want to be my child's best friend." I respond to that: God doesn't need you to be your child's best friend. Today on earth there are 6.4 billion people who can be your child's friend. But only one person can be their mama, and only one person can be their daddy. Above anything else, you need to be the adult God wants you to be for that child. And if you do that, eventually you will be their best friend. But, right now, you need to do what's right for them. Because, ultimately, God didn't give children to schools or even to churches. He gave them to parents.

Allan is right. We caution that this doesn't mean you can't be *close* to your children, being candid with certain intimate information that you choose judiciously to share so as to encourage, guide, and admonish them. But the key is to use discernment. Tell it for the right reason—in other words, as a parent, not as a friend.

Ron Jenson said:

The home can be a climate where kids either hunger to want to be their best or not want to be their best. I think there need to be tough love and discipline, but there always needs to be grace. I remember one time when my son Matt and I were soaking in our Jacuzzi. He was pouring out his heart about how he was failing in an area of his life. I went, "You've got to be kidding. Let me tell you my stories." I just started telling him story after story of failures in my life.

I had mentioned some of these in passing during earlier talks, but I think they'd gone over his head—kids look up to their parents and think we don't fail. I told him what I'd learned from these failures, how they'd changed me. I told him the key is *to fail forward.* He was old enough by the time of this conversation to learn from my disclosures. And, of course, I didn't tell him *everything.* If he'd been younger, I might have seemed like I was bringing myself down to his level, being a kid too. But this gave him insight into manhood. It made him less afraid of failure, more motivated to be his best.

Many people talked to us about bonding, parent to child. Randy Pope said:

We always had a goal for our kids to think, *I've got cool parents,* so they would want to be with us, not only for the sheer enjoyment but for the teaching opportunities. To accomplish that meant doing a lot of play with them, letting them see me when I'm real and goofy and crazy. I remember lying down with my son when he was six or seven. Somebody I knew who had little children had recently died, and it got me to thinking. I asked my son, "If something happened and the Lord took me home, and then you met a good buddy a few weeks later who asked what I was like, what would you say? How would you describe me?"

He pondered that for a while. I'm thinking and hoping he'll come up with something like "man of God," "spiritual," "wise," whatever. Finally, he came out with it: "I'd tell him you were nutsy." At first, I thought, *Oh, man, "nutsy," that's what he thinks of me, that I'm nuts, crazy, goofy.* Then it dawned on me. That was his way of saying, "I like being with you. I'm a kid, and I like nutsy people."

DEVELOP A STRUCTURED METHOD OF PRAYING FOR YOUR CHILD

Over and over in our interviews we heard from parents who prayed for their children, not only during their growing-up years but often before they were born. (One man told us how he prayed for his children even before he was married!) In each case, one common denominator stood out: they used some sort of structured format, perhaps a journal or notebook where they could keep detailed notes of prayer requests, prayers answered. The structure provided motivation and consistency. Plus it was an encouragement to see how God was working in the lives of their children. Here's how one woman used hers.

Julie Taylor said:

I actually began prayer journaling in college. By the time I began having children, it was a well-established habit. When each child was born, I began a prayer journal with the child's name on the front and a few Scripture verses to claim for him or her. I can't say how I chose the verses other than I felt they were about parenting. With Brent I began every day to write down something that I was thankful for about him or had a prayer request about. It could be anything . . . helping him get to sleep, for example. In the beginning, I'm not talking about fifteen lines of prayer over a child, maybe just two or three. Then I always went back and looked over previous requests. If I realized the prayer had been answered, I wrote in how.

As the child grew older, my prayer requests might be related more to character-development issues. I asked the Lord to give me a Bible verse to go with the issue. Maybe I was praying against the anger in Brent or the stubbornness in Becca's heart. This process kept building on itself. It's full of praises as well as requests. And as they matured, the prayers took on more depth, such as praying for them to take a leadership role, praying for boldness in sharing their faith. The journals are loose-leaf notebooks, and I keep buying more pages. After several years, I remove some of the older pages and put them in a box marked with that child's name. Some things I'm still praying for.

MODEL GOOD BEHAVIOR FOR YOUR CHILDREN

The Bible has much to say about how to treat one another with caring, respect, dignity, love. But what does this mean in our modern-day context? How can we teach this to our children so they can apply it to their lives? One way is in response to the coarseness of our society where manners have almost gone out the window. Holding a chair for a lady? Who does that sort of thing anymore? Well, Mike Stabile knows.

First, I should tell you that I grew up as kind of a barbarian . . . I didn't have good manners or social graces. My wardrobe was tee shirts and jerseys and sneakers. I didn't treat women very well either. I was from an ethnicity where men often had the attitude that women were basically there for them, never the other way around. That's how I was raised.

When I started dating Pam, she opened up a whole new world for me. For example, when we pulled up to the curb on our first date, I got out, but she stayed in the car. I walked back to the car and said, "Let's go." She just sat there quietly, and I realized she wanted me to open the door for her. So I opened the door.

Then we went to the movie theater. I paid for the ticket and walked in. No Pam. I looked out through the glass doors. There she stood on the other side. Again, I had fumbled, just charging ahead. I hadn't taken care of her. As our relationship progressed, she shared with me that she had prayed for a man who would love her and treasure her and respect her. This was a big lesson to me. I had to learn how to show her that I had those attitudes.

When we married and had daughters, we decided that one way to convey respect was to treat the girls this way, to show them a standard that they should expect for themselves. It would also help them value themselves as women. So we had these "dates." The girls and I started this practice we called Daddy-Daughter

Day. I opened the door for them; I pulled out their chairs for them. When they got up from the table to go to the rest room, I was sure to stand up. I remember one of my daughters saying, "You know, Dad, guys have no manners whatsoever. They don't know how to respect the ladies. You've got to teach them how to respect you." That's how it had been with Pam and me. It was so interesting to hear that.

Plug into a Strong Community of Faith

It takes a full crew to launch a space shuttle. Many people we spoke to said they sought people to be on their team as they raised their children. And what better place than the church? There you can find accountability partners, people who will be role models to your children, people who can keep an eye out for them when you aren't around. And there's where your children can see you doing some of the foundational things that will make a lifelong impression.

Allan Taylor said:

Make sure you and your children are in God's house on the day of worship. Make sure your kids see you with a Bible in your hand. Make sure they see you on your knees before God. Make sure they see you put your offering in the plate. Make sure they see you singing praises and hymns. It's one thing for us to take our kids to church; it's another thing for them to see us *worship* at church. And, most of all, make sure you get the Word of God into the hearts of your children. Just as we tenderize a steak, His Word tenderizes the hearts of our children.

Keep Reading, Parent . . .

Of course, you have to raise only one child to be a blue-ribbon expert on child rearing, in our opinion. But the twenty or so couples we spoke to represent at least sixty children, plus a couple dozen grandchildren. Multiplication: that's what growing the kingdom is about, isn't it? It's producing one generation after another that trusts the Lord and serves Him. It's helping your children discover their lives' missions. It's teaching them to share Christ effectively and with confidence.

No one does a better job of putting flesh on what it means to be *on mission* than the Parrott family. You'll read more about them in the principles section, chapters 10 through 25, but we'll give you a peek into their lives now.

Mike and Tracey Parrott challenged each of their children to establish a top ten list. No, it wasn't like David Letterman's. It was a list of fellow students whom they wanted to share Christ with, kids they knew from school or the neighborhood who didn't have a personal relationship with the Lord. The idea was to be deliberate and intentional about it—which is the definition of what we call being *on mission*. Mike and Tracey trained the kids in effective ways to tell their friends how God had changed their lives. Periodically they checked on their kids' progress with really using the top ten lists as a game plan for witnessing.

We'll tell you just one success story—about Luke. Mike had been praying for the kids' diligence with their lists. He realized that by the end of the first three months of his sophomore year, almost every kid on Luke's list had come to know Christ. *What a success!* thought Mike. And as a dad he was tempted to want to take over discipling Luke's friends himself, forming a Bible study. It wasn't a far-out idea, considering he and Tracey were actually writing the curriculum they were using to teach their kids techniques for sharing their faith. But God told Mike, "No, this is going to be Luke's group. Your role is to motivate him to do it."

Mike felt comfortable trusting his son with this responsibility, because Luke had been faithful with daily quiet times and journaling since seventh grade. So Mike asked Luke, "With all these friends of yours who have come to know Christ as Savior, who's going to help them grow?" Luke answered, "I think I can help them with that." Mike answered, "I think you can too." And Mike was pleased to find that, sure enough, Luke followed through, often using his father's study material. And so Luke, just in his teens, became a multiplier of the faithful for the kingdom.

It's not easy to be a family like the Parrotts. Parenting is hard work. But *on mission* parenting is possible—and so satisfying! Especially if we recognize the unique qualities of our children and play to their strengths.

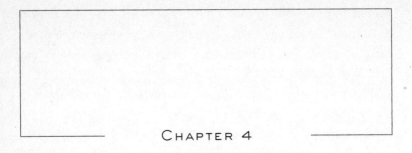

CHAPTER 4

BEGINNING WITH
THE END IN MIND

Several years ago Bob ran into his friend Pat Morley at a conference in Orlando. Pat took one look at Bob's drawn and weary face and nailed it: Bob was overworked. He had traveled too much, spoken too often, and met too many people. He was pulled in all directions and was ready to crash and burn.

Pat, being a friend who, at that moment, had more perspective than the worn-out Bob, got straight to the point: "Bob, look around. How many of these people do you think will come to your funeral when you die?"

Sobered and shell-shocked, Bob had to admit, "Probably none. Everybody's too busy! We've all got more conferences to attend!"

With an encouraging smile, Pat said, "Why don't you begin with the end in mind? I'd like to challenge you to do something you probably haven't done. Go home and take some time to be quiet. Then write out what you would like your obituary to say when you die. Put into words what you hope will be the lasting impact of your life."

Why don't you begin with the end in mind? That challenge began a revealing journey in Bob's life that's still going on. Now, instead of saying yes to every opportunity, Bob evaluates each one with the end result in mind: What's really important? Will this have a lasting impact? And what brings significance and not just success?

These are questions that have resonated with us as a couple, because they strike at the core of what's really important to us as adults, as marriage partners, and as parents. When it's all said and done, we want to live lives that make a difference in the lives of others. And as we scrutinize the landscape of our hectic schedules, one thing becomes very clear: what better place to impact others than in the lives of our very own kids?

So why don't we all begin parenting with the end in mind? For our kids' lives to be successful—by being significant—we have to look ourselves in the mirror and ask some tough questions: What choices do our kids see us making? What kind of role models are we becoming for choosing significance over success? Or to put it more bluntly: to give our kids the best shot at making *their lives* count, are we as parents doing everything within our power to make *our lives* count?

ARE YOU MAKING YOUR LIFE COUNT?

One of the first questions we pose is this: *are you making your life count?* Most people want to leave an imprint—to leave things and people better than they found them. Yet we fear that the impact of our lives could more resemble a fist in water than a handprint in cement. The handprint is there to stay, but the ripples in the water soon settle and smooth as though the fist had never been there. We all dread the notion that in the end, our lives might not count for much.

We discovered how widespread is that fear of failure to make a difference when we were conducting research for *Made to Count.* You may find it a useful book for your own preparation as you launch your kids into the futures God has planned for them.

But don't break into a cold sweat. What your kids don't need are perfect parents. What they do need are *teachable* parents! And by the way, maybe you're a bit intimidated by this job of being a parent. Perhaps your own background was painful or flawed enough that you secretly wonder if you could possibly have what it takes to do this job.

If so, maybe the following stories will help.

"What Do You Want with That?"

Several years ago, in the picturesque tidewater basin of the Virginia coast, three young boys were born in stairstep fashion. In a period of three years, all three had entered this brave new world. But not every child who steps into the world finds a pleasant or easy reception awaiting him. For these three, the journey ahead would be anything but smooth sailing.

The father, who was involved in the military, was an alcoholic. While some people become humorous when they have too much to drink, others take on a less-than-pleasant demeanor. This father happened to be in the latter category.

Soon after the third son was born, the mother was stricken with cancer. Life became much more than she could handle. She was striving to take care of three children all under the age of three, she was battling cancer, and she was trying to cope with an alcoholic husband and father to her children. By the time her youngest was eleven months old, she gave up the fight and died.

The father then found himself responsible not only for a military career, but also for raising three small children. Sometimes he was up to the task, sometimes not. The responsibility and demands were more than he wanted to face. Compared to raising three preschoolers, the military was a breeze!

Also, the responsibilities got in the way of him enjoying a good drink now and then . . . and "now" was always preferable. When he got tired of the boys, he threw them out to another home—any home—that would take them off his hands and give him a break. When he needed to feel good about himself, or to look respectable, he grabbed them back. Thus the cycle began: he handed off the kids to others to get some breathing room, then he dragged the kids back and forced himself into the role of a parent.

The cycle repeated until finally, having had all the fun he could stand, he threw the boys out for what was the last time. The three were passed from hand to hand and house to house, all the way from Virginia to southern Illinois, where they found themselves deposited in another home willing to take them in—at least for a short while.

Meantime, a young couple in southern Illinois had suffered through three miscarriages and one stillbirth. The last had been especially traumatic because the baby had been discovered dead in the mother's womb. Physicians had not diagnosed it early enough, so peritonitis had set in, which poisoned the womb. The doctors had done well to pull the mother through the trauma, but in the end they told her there was no hope for any more children in the future.

Hearing of the little fellows' plight, the young couple found their way to the home where the youngsters had been staying. They knocked on the front door. "We understand you have some little boys here who are in need of a home. We thought we'd come and see if we could be of any help." The gruff lady who opened the door quickly indicated that the two older boys had been taken by a couple, leaving only the youngest. "The brat's in the back! Take a look if you want to. It's up to you." With that she wheeled around and walked away.

Making their way through the house, they came to a back bedroom where the little guy was playing. It was obvious he hadn't been washed in days. He was sitting in diapers that had long needed changing.

What was worse, the little fellow was covered with a skin disease called *impetigo,* which creates body sores that ooze with a puslike discharge. In other words, the boy was a ghastly mess.

Not to be deterred, the young wife gathered him up in her arms with no thought to the stains that immediately appeared on her new dress. "We'll take him! We'll take him!" she said. Shrugging her shoulders, the homeowner said, "Do what you like." And she let them out of the house.

They arrived at the local doctor's office and set the little boy on the examining table. When the doctor entered the room and saw the dirty and diseased child, the comment that came rolling out of his mouth before he could catch it was, "My God! What do you want with that?" Some people discount anyone who doesn't have beauty, brains, or bucks. This doctor was no exception.

But the young wife answered, "We're willing to take him, because if somebody like us doesn't, he'll never have the chance to become what God created him to be."

Intriguing story? Sound like a novel? Expecting to see it in an upcoming movie? You've just read the beginning of Bob's life.

And the story doesn't end there. Neither of Bob's adoptive parents had finished high school. His adoptive father had been an illegitimate child whose biological father had rejected him. Raised by an alcoholic step-grandfather and grandmother, Bob's adoptive dad never had a role model for what a home of loving acceptance and affirmation was all about. So it's easy to understand why this brand-new dad often faltered when it came to knowing how to express love and affirmation to Bob.

His adoptive mother, however, was gifted with compassion and mercy and was constantly ready to give herself away to those in need. She encouraged Bob with ideas such as these:

- God has a special plan for you, and He's giving us the joy of being a part of it.

- God created you for a purpose, and we're committed to helping you find it.

- God knew your future even before you were born, and He's got a plan for you to fulfill!

And when in the journey Bob became impatient, his mother said, "Be patient, because God's not finished with you yet!"

LEAVE IT TO BEAVER HOME

Cheryl, on the other hand, was born into the ideal *Leave It to Beaver* household. Her dad went to an executive job every day, and her mom met her dad each evening at the door having just bathed and changed into a fashionable dress complete with pearl necklace. Each evening the family sat together at a meal. Her great-grandfather had even come from the old country to plant a church in Nebraska. Their lives included activities at the golf club, and her father was treasurer at the local Lutheran church.

Is this a picture of Ward and June Cleaver, or what?

In addition, Cheryl's parents constantly provided encouragement, telling her of their belief that her future was bright and that she had been born with a purpose. Life was God's gift to her, and what she did with it would be her gift to Him.

There you have it. Your authors grew up in two radically different circumstances, but what they had in common was just what they needed: the message that God had plans for their lives and the encouragement to seek His plans and fulfill their destinies. Despite the huge discrepancy in the educational levels and socioeconomic environments of the two sets of parents, this vital message was communicated. Our parents were committed to helping us, their children, make our lives count.

The same could be true of you. Your childhood may have been wonderful, or it may have been lousy. Whatever it was, don't let it limit you. Don't use it as an excuse. Remember that you are responsible for launching your own children, and the success or failure of that does not depend on your own upbringing. It depends on how you start over with a clean slate in raising them.

Do You Have What It Takes?

As you can see from our stories and as we've mentioned, God doesn't need perfect parents; He needs teachable parents. Give yourself a test by answering these questions:

- Do you want your children to make a significant impact in their world?

- Would you love to see God bless their lives in ways you never imagined possible?

- Would you love to watch them focus on making an eternal impact by what they do—starting now?

- Would you love to share some experiences and projects that they will remember long after you're gone?

- Would you love to build into their lives biblically based principles that will help them evaluate what's really important and what's not, what really lasts and what doesn't?

- Do you want to see your kids fulfill the very purposes for which they were born—to see them understand that God designed them for specific destinies?

If these questions resonate deep within you, then, yes, parent, you have what it takes. In fact, God wouldn't have entrusted into your care the children you have unless He knew you could provide them with the Mission Control they need for a successful launch.

CHAPTER 5

UNIQUE KIDS FOR UNIQUE MISSIONS

Do you ever wonder why God doesn't bless us with kids who are more alike, just to make life a little easier? When we started our family, we weren't ready for just how different our kids would be from one another. And, frankly, our expectations were pretty naive too.

Adoptive parents with very little extended family raised Bob, while Cheryl grew up with a brother and a horde of extended family within easy driving distance. Bob thought kids came potty trained, and Cheryl had never changed a diaper in her life. And we both *just knew* our children would be different from everyone else's: quiet and orderly in public, not fussy, easygoing because they'd had eight or nine hours of sleep, and, of course, *never* demanding.

Wow! What a surprise when each child came into the world with a mind of his or her own.

HERE'S CHRISTY!

Christy, our oldest, came into this world with a gleam in her eye, smoking a cigar and demanding, "Who *used to be* in charge here?"

Right away, we knew we were in for a challenge. But we thought we had probably brought this on ourselves since both of us have dominant personalities. *Strong-willed* was the modus operandi for both of us, and while we never considered divorce, murder was a temptation more than once. Those who know us best think it's a miracle that we've not just survived, but thrived for more than thirty years of marriage. So we came to realize that at times in life, the chickens just come home to roost.

Christy arrived competitive, driven, determined, and ready to take charge. And she wanted her space until she was ready to have people in her world. Often in the mornings when Christy was still in the crib, we heard her cooing, babbling, and making wonderful noises to entertain herself. That is, until we entered her room. And then the Dead Man's Stare would glare at us through the slats, telling us to get out of her space until she was ready.

We were attempting to teach her sportsmanship and fairness by age four. Her brother, Bryan, had also joined our family and was a year old. One night we were playing the game Uno. Suddenly Christy looked at us and said, "Don't you hear Bryan crying? I think he needs you." We fell for it, hook, line, and sinker. After we returned from checking on our sleeping one-year-old, we discovered that Christy had loaded her hand with Draw Four cards!

When Bob was working with a neighborhood crew to landscape our community's entrance, he heard a group of children declaring what they would be when they grew up. "A doctor," said one. "An astronaut," another proclaimed. "A fireman!" a tow-headed boy shouted. And then Christy spoke up: "Me, I'm going to be king of the world!"

And today, in her twenties, she's still driven and overcoming.

She's bounced back from a lengthy health problem. In a tough economy, she's found a great new job within weeks of losing her former job when that company closed its doors. In her spare time she takes less-than-promising soccer teams and molds them into contenders for league titles.

MEET BRYAN!

Bryan, on the other hand, came into life with a smile on his face, an adaptable spirit, and a dry wit, ready to ease everyone's stress and defuse tension. He has a steel-trap memory. As we served in churches and held baptismal services, we heard Bryan mumbling to himself and asked what he was doing. "I'm memorizing their names so that the next time I see them I'll know who they are."

He's great with detail. He has an amazing ability to work complicated processes and retain large amounts of information.

We took Bryan, age ten, to tennis lessons just knowing he would become a star and take care of us in our old age. Picking him up one sunny afternoon, Cheryl asked him how things had gone.

"Fine," was the simple reply.

"Did you win?" asked Cheryl.

"Well, I won the first set. And then I realized that the other boy hadn't won anything, so I let him win the next two."

So much for the killer instinct, and so much for having a tennis pro taking care of us in our old age! No wonder Bryan is so popular with his friends. They say he feels like your favorite pair of shoes: always comfortable.

NOW COMES ASHLEY!

And then there is our social butterfly, our youngest, Ashley. She loves people, and she tackles every experience as an opportunity to build relationships. We said all through her school years that if every assignment had been a group project, she would have been a straight-A student. Her teachers told us year after year that Ashley was the child they counted on to reach out and be friendly to any new children and make them feel welcome.

Now that she's an adult, that attitude of caring so much for others manifests itself in surprising ways. For example, Cheryl and Ashley went shopping together. Cheryl, who is task-oriented, dealt with a salesclerk in what she considered to be a straightforward manner. But Ashley's take on the exchange was, "Mom, you were rude to that salesperson!"

"How in the world was I rude? I just took care of what I needed."

"But, Mom, you didn't ask how her day had been first. You need to make her feel good and let her know you're interested in her!"

We both admit that Ashley has helped us become more sensitive to others and to their feelings, even when we're with strangers. She loves people and can light up like a light bulb when she walks into a room. We expect God to guide her into a career path that builds on her gift of reaching out and helping people.

WIRED BY THE CREATOR

The personality differences we identify in our kids help us as parents understand that the Creator wired each child uniquely for a calling and a purpose. We see that He has handed us three challenges, and the question becomes: will we encourage or squelch who they are? Because, honestly, sometimes our kids' differences just seem to push our buttons. (You can identify, can't you?)

And sometimes their differences don't seem much like a gift, but more a source of clashes and sore spots. Yet each of our kids has taught us a great deal about life and about the variety of personalities that God creates and provides within each family. Frankly, accepting these differences and adapting our parenting techniques accordingly were challenges at first. We found that we had to be open to learn as well as ready to teach. We wanted our responses to say volumes to them about their worth. And we had to believe that God created each of them with a special bent for a specific mission.

Proverbs 22:6 says: "Train up a child in the way he should go, / And when he is old he will not depart from it" (NKJV). This verse carries at least two messages. It conveys the responsibility we have to train our children in the ways of God. It also highlights the need to train them according to their individual gifts and personalities, as no two children are the same. God wants us to parent our children in the way that fits who they are, trusting His creation of them and His plans for their lives.

PROVIDING WINGS

As we build into our children their *roots* in life, we've already established that the ultimate goal is to give them *wings*. But that doesn't happen overnight or in five easy steps. So what can a parent do to positively prepare their kids for future successful launches? We intend to answer that with suggestions of practical helps for parents to employ without adding a million to-do's to your daily list. Here are three ideas.

IDEA #1

One simple step is to take time *every day* to tell your children how special they are and how you are convinced that God created them for a special purpose. Don't think they know this by intuition or that they will simply pick it up in the friendly atmosphere of home. Kids need to be told. And the best ways to convey this message are through touch and eye contact.

Even when your child is very young, begin communicating this important message. Find a time each day to put your hand on his or to place your arm around her shoulders, and while looking your child straight in the eye, state clearly how special you're convinced your child is "because God made you for a specific purpose in life." Your gentle touch builds into their young hearts a sense of security, acceptance, affirmation, and support. And the eye-to-eye contact fills their emotional reservoir. You can see it happening right in front of your eyes!

Idea #2

When your children are old enough to read, write each one a personal letter. Use that communication opportunity to express characteristics you appreciate about them. Express how these characteristics are evidence that God is preparing them for His very special purposes in life. Focus on character qualities about *who they are,* more than merely *what they do.* This is a great time to build into your children an understanding that *being* is more significant than *doing.*

Focus on qualities such as a sense of humor, the integrity you observe in them that allows you to take their word to the bank, their sense of fairness when they play, the encouragement they express to others, and the friendship skills they use to include family and friends in whatever they do. The more specific your comments, the better.

Perhaps they are proving to be quite adept socially by fitting into groups of people and adapting comfortably in their new classes at the beginning of a school year. Maybe one of your children needs to hear that you value his can-do spirit and willingness to jump into the middle of a responsibility and make things work. Another child may have a quiet and gentle demeanor that makes her easy to spend time with. Or maybe you have a child who fell down in the race of life but has shown a remarkable ability to bounce back and keep on going. Whatever their strengths—friendliness, a positive attitude, resilience—let each one know you appreciate and value those traits and believe they are all part of God's plan for his or her life. Convey the message that you will help nurture these traits. Their futures depend on it.

Idea #3

Take opportunities to bless your children. The idea of blessing appears throughout Scripture and illustrates the powerful impact of parents' investments in their children's futures.

The best way we have found to bless our children is literally to pray Scripture over them. When they're still at home, you can do this as they go to bed, around a meal table, while they sleep, or any time of your choosing. It conveys the granting and endowing of God's good graces and wonderful favor. In Scripture this most often was accomplished through a verbal spoken word and the laying on of hands.

BLESSING YOUR CHILD

Here's an example of using Scripture to bless your child. Psalm 19:7–12 in *The Message* reads:

> The revelation of GOD is whole
> and pulls our lives together.
> The signposts of GOD are clear
> and point out the right road.
> The life-maps of GOD are right,
> showing the way to joy.
> The directions of GOD are plain
> and easy on the eyes.
> God's reputation is twenty-four-carat gold,
> with a lifetime guarantee.
> The decisions of GOD are accurate
> down to the nth degree.
> God's Word is better than a diamond,
> better than a diamond set between emeralds.
> . . . There's more: God's Word warns us of danger
> and directs us to hidden treasure.

Otherwise how will we find our way?
Or know when we play the fool?

Find such a passage that would be a blessing for your child, then simply pray to the Lord, inserting your child's name where appropriate. It could sound something like this:

Lord, we pray for [child's name] that [he or she] will always understand that Your Word is whole and complete and is the very thing that pulls our lives together.

May [child's name] always see that the signposts of Your Word give clarity for [him or her] to walk the right road as [he or she] grows and matures.

Father, thank You for giving [child's name] a life-map that will always be right and for showing [him or her] the way to joy by trusting Your Word.

May [child's name] see Your directions as always plain and clear, and may [he or she] value them more than money, precious jewelry, or possessions.

May [child's name] constantly be blessed by seeing the accuracy of everything You say.

And, Lord, please warn [child's name] of danger, direct [him or her] to unexpected blessings, and make the way safe and clear.

Bless [child's name] in everything [he or she] does.

The Bible is filled with passages that parents can choose to pray over their kids as blessings. Just a few other examples:

- Don't let anyone look down on you because you are young, but set an example for the believers in speech, in life, in love, in faith and in purity. (1 Timothy 4:12)

- For the eyes of the LORD range throughout the earth to strengthen those whose hearts are fully committed to him. (2 Chronicles 16:9)
- Oh, that you would bless me and enlarge my territory! Let your hand be with me, and keep me from harm so that I will be free from pain. (The prayer of Jabez, 1 Chronicles 4:10)

Imagine the power of your prayers of blessing in the lives of your kids and the comfort they will feel as they hear you say the words. They'll learn that the prayers of righteous moms and dads accomplish much!

Every night our friend David Doverspike has slipped in to pray with each child, specifically asking God to bless him or her with grace, insight, peace, and humor and that they would become people of character, compassion, and concern. David found that about five or ten minutes with the guys is about all they can take, while the girls are willing to go a little longer. Sometimes he uses Scriptures to guide his prayers:

- Ephesians 6:1–3: Help the children to understand that honoring parents is where God's blessing begins.
- 2 Corinthians 6:14: Grant them Christian spouses, and be working in those future spouses' lives even though we don't know who they are or what the future holds.
- 1 Thessalonians 4:11–12: Bless them in their work, both schoolwork as children and occupations as adults.
- Ephesians 6:1–4 and 1 Timothy 5:8: Help me use these Scriptures as a model for my parenting.
- 1 Corinthians 13: Let their hearts be characterized by this kind of love.
- James 2: Keep them from being prejudiced.
- The book of Proverbs: Grant them wisdom and the ability and grace to accept Your wisdom. (Our friend David has

regularly shared key principles from the book of Proverbs with his kids.)

Here are some verses to assure you of God's readiness to hear your prayers of blessing on behalf of your children.

- Call to me and I will answer you and tell you great and unsearchable things you do not know. (Jeremiah 33:3)
- This is the confidence we have in approaching God: that if we ask anything according to his will, he hears us. And if we know that he hears us—whatever we ask—we know that we have what we asked of him. (1 John 5:14–15)

Listen to the testimony of one father who has put such a plan into action:

Each evening at bedtime, I would lay my hands on the head of each of my children and speak a blessing that appears in Numbers 6:24–26, adding at the end the words "In the name of the Father, and of the Son, and of the Holy Spirit," and personalizing it to each child by including his or her name.

It was that simple. We just spoke the same blessing to our children each night. And they came to depend on it as a token of security and a sign of their parents' continuing love for them.[1]

Think how pleasing your prayers of blessing will be to the Lord as you pray His Word right back to Him in the presence of your children!

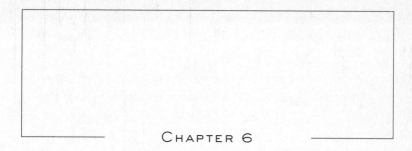

CHAPTER 6

BUT WHAT ABOUT ME? MY SPOUSE ISN'T ON BOARD . . .

No need to read this chapter if (1) you and your spouse are 100 percent in agreement all the time; (2) your level of commitment and involvement in launching your kids to be *on mission* is absolutely always in sync; and (3) you know everything you need to know about what makes the opposite sex—namely, the spouse with whom you are raising a family—tick.

For the *very few of you* still with us (picture us smiling!), what you'll read in this chapter is our best thinking on spouses who are not totally on board. They may be too busy or they may lack understanding of the need. They may have issues from their pasts that prevent them from contributing as much as you need or want. They may be harboring out-of-date attitudes. Sadly, they may talk the talk but not walk the walk—or in some cases, they may not have the heart commitment to Christ that you have. And too often in our society (including the Christian community, where the divorce rate runs about as high as in the non-Christian community), they simply may not be there physically.

In short, spouses can be (or seem to be) AWOL for many reasons. We add "seem to be" because sometimes we put a type of unhealthy pressure on our spouses that psychologists might say drives them away. But—bottom line—*if it feels to you* as if your spouse is unsupportive on the level of Christian parenting you want to achieve, then that's the reality you're dealing with.

We hope our vulnerability in this chapter does not make you squirm. Our desire is to help. And to encourage. As we say throughout this book, God does not need perfect parents in order to add another generation to His kingdom. He needs parents who are willing to make a few adjustments, to try some new ideas, to grow themselves so that their kids can find their wings.

Here, instead of blending our voices as we do in most sections of the book, we will share individually from our own points of view. Bob's perspective on husbands comes first, followed by what Cheryl has to say about being a wife and trying to launch *on mission* kids.

Bob on Husbands

Perhaps you're a wife who wants to make a focused effort to help your kids find God's plans for their lives, but you have a dilemma: your husband isn't on the same page. Maybe he's just not sure about all this "spiritual stuff," and you don't understand why. For you, it seems obvious and straightforward that spiritual roots are necessary for an effective set of future "wings." But he seems to drag his feet, not buy in, and at times resists spiritual matters, whether it be with the kids or even with you.

Let's talk about what makes guys tick—and what you can do to help.

The Performance Factor

It's likely your husband grew up in a culture in which a young or grown man was evaluated by performance. From early on boys are taught to be tough, to give life their all, and to squelch emotion in order to accomplish their goals and achieve success. Maybe they heard: "Come on, big boys don't cry. Suck it up, and get back in the game. You're a man now, so get in there and be tough. If there's no pain, there's no gain!" (Have you ever noticed that the ones saying this are never the ones experiencing the pain?)

And so it is that boys are raised in a culture where *how they perform* is the measure of most things. Add to that one other tyrannical master: the opinions of others. Most boys and young men want others to think they're tough, they're producers equal to the task and not quitters. They hear: "What will Coach think if you don't . . . ? Are you gonna let down the team by not carrying your weight?" And even if others don't impose the expectation, it can often have a more ruthless origin: the heart of the young man himself. Self-imposed performance expectations can be healthy, but they can also be hard taskmasters.

That's why if you listen to conversations between men and conversations between women, you find a very different focus. Men immediately go to what they *do*. They focus on their work, their jobs, their titles, their recreational activities, or even their past accomplishments of schooling, degrees, athletic prowess, or job experience. Women go to who they *are* as mothers, caregivers; they are relationship-driven and social. Women focus on what they can *share* together, while men focus on what they can *do* together. Give most women five minutes, and they'll be talking intimate, personal details about their lives, dreams, concerns, and passions. Check in on men twenty minutes after a conversation has begun, and they probably haven't moved passed recent game scores, where each of them is working, and what they did last weekend.

Ah, diversity is the spice of life!

MEN'S GREATEST FEAR

This leads to a significant dilemma for many men. Because *performance* is so central to the development of boys into men, performance affects them as they become husbands and fathers. Most feel they are on a stage, expected to give the performance of a lifetime. They feel they are constantly being judged by what they do or don't do—and how well they perform in these domesticated roles in a family.

Here's what our friend Shaunti Feldhahn wrote in her book *For Women Only:*

> A man's inner vulnerability about his performance often stems from his conviction that at all times he is being watched and judged. In my . . . survey, I found that no matter how secure the men looked on the outside, two-thirds admitted being insecure about others' opinion of them . . . [There was] also the internal realization that since they don't always know what they are doing, they are just one mess-up away from being found out.[1]

She added this insight: "Many men feel . . . inadequate at home."[2]

That tracks with what a Christian psychiatrist told us several years ago: a man's most significant fear is being inadequate. Stop and think about it for a moment. How often do you see on television, read in books, or hear in your day-to-day life that men are afraid of being inadequate financially, professionally, sexually, emotionally? You see it everywhere you turn. That fear of inadequacy can be overwhelming to a man, and one of the easiest ways for him to deal with it is *to avoid the circumstances that reveal inadequacy*. And that's as true in the spiritual realm as it is in the occupational or athletic realms.

PULLING BACK THE CURTAIN

I'll tell you how it was for me.

Having my mom die when I was eleven months old and being

left to an alcoholic dad was a tough beginning on my road of life. On the one hand, I felt huge rejection, but on the other hand, I sensed I was fortunate to have a couple step forward and take the risk of adoption by taking me into their home.

Although neither of my adoptive parents finished high school due to family and personal issues, they gave me a strong home where I knew I was loved and valued. They labored hard to give me the opportunity to be the first one in either of their families to attend and graduate from college.

My adoptive mom was one of the most caring, giving people I've ever been around. At the drop of a hat, she was off and engaged in helping someone in trouble. If there were two pieces of pecan pie at dinner, she made sure that my dad and I each had one . . . and naturally, she did without. That sort of giving was in the DNA of her personality.

My adoptive dad was a strong, hardworking construction type who operated heavy equipment. He was a man's man with biceps as big as my thighs. His beginnings were tough. In a drunken rage, his step-granddad often forced him to sleep overnight in the barn. Not being allowed back into the house during the night caused my dad heartbreaking loneliness and terror—a terror further fueled when he was bitten by rats and had to endure weeks of painful antirabies shots.

It was my mom and a pastor who introduced my dad to Christ. But with his background, Dad never felt comfortable being much of a spiritual leader in our home. I don't think I ever saw my dad pray with my mom. On Sundays Mom and I left the house for Sunday school and church. Later Dad slipped into the service, taking a seat about three rows from the back, then he bolted at the last amen to smoke a cigarette on the church sidewalk. While he was a good man and a great provider, we never once had a devotional time as a family.

Imagine my quandary when suddenly, after falling in love with

Cheryl and getting married, I found myself a husband. Not only that, I had sensed a calling into the ministry and headed with my new bride to seminary. That's where I heard about how important and "natural" family devotional times were and how every husband ought to be leading them every day. Yet I'd never had one modeled for me in my lifetime. I didn't know where to begin, what to do, or how to make it work.

Praying with Cheryl was one of the scariest things I could imagine. Not because of Cheryl—she was great. It was because of an expectation I had built in my mind of the need to be a "spiritual giant" in order to lead prayer successfully. And by then, I had discovered that you can pray publicly and sound pretty spiritual, because nobody knows what you are twenty-four hours a day. But when you try to do that with your wife—who sees you at the best of times and the worst of times—you are vulnerable and exposed if you try to sound too spiritual. So I found that often the easiest thing to do was avoid it.

When our kids came along, fatherhood added a whole new dimension of inadequacy to the idea of leading family devotions. As they grew old enough to understand what was going on, you should have seen their faces: they rolled back their eyes as if going into a coma, or they kicked each other under the table just to relieve their boredom, or they stared at me, which I took to mean: "Get this over with before I turn into a sphinx."

What made matters worse for me was that every time I heard Christians talk about the importance of family devotions, they made it sound as if their families exuded a heavenly glow, sitting quietly around the table with reverently folded hands. In summary, they were angels turning their houses into Westminster Abbey. And, of course, at the end of the study, their children clamored for more. Since I never got anywhere close to that type of response—in fact, not even in the same universe—I can remember feeling totally inadequate, yet ashamed to admit to anyone that I was struggling.

Since then, I've gotten to know lots of Christian leaders person- ally, and many have confided that family devotions aren't as easy as some make it sound. The majority admitted to having kids with the "disinterest gene." *Why didn't you tell me that earlier?* I wanted to ask each one. They had no idea how liberating it would have been to know that I wasn't by myself in feeling inadequate, that I didn't have to be Billy Graham to make it work, and that there were helps to learn how to get it done.

I even learned that when it came to workable family devotions, many held the time to ten or fifteen minutes. Before that, I'd been left with the impression I should sustain their interest in Bible study for thirty to forty-five minutes. (And honestly, sometimes even I was drift- ing into a coma!) Also, many talked of family devotions as seizing those "teachable moments" that naturally occur and helping their kids understand how they relate to biblical principles—something I was often doing. I just hadn't recognized those counted as devotional times!

Well, I've come a long way in my growth and thankfully have learned that God is not a performance-focused God. Instead He is a God of relationship who wants me to be the very best I can be and to have my spiritual leadership literally be an outpouring of my personal relationship with Him. And frankly, I'm still in the process of grow- ing there. Some days I still lapse back into a performance mentality.

I'm thankful that Cheryl has loved me enough to help me grow, to affirm me as a man, and to assure me that I'm not inadequate. She has learned a critical truth that every wife should know: the greatest fear of every man is being inadequate!

So What's a Woman to Do?

You're a wife who wants her husband to join in with a spiritual focus in the family, especially when it comes to passing it on to kids. What can you do?

Regularly tell your husband how thankful you are for him. Notice I said, "how thankful you are for *him*," not for *what he does*. It's an easy thing to subconsciously support a performance orientation by complimenting actions more than attitudes and aptitudes. Try to adjust that in the next few days, and I promise you'll see results.

Focus on character more than conduct. Find two or three qualities of character in your husband that you appreciate and respect. Maybe you notice he consistently respects people's time, so he is punctual. Maybe you notice he thinks of others before himself. Tell him you see these qualities. Find credible ways to build him up and let him know that he is adequate in your eyes.

Don't beat him over the head with spiritual issues. Men recoil when they feel their mates are lecturing or instructing them. They also resent being compared with someone else's husband "who is doing it right." Instead, make positive comments about what God is doing in *your* life as a wife and mother and what you see Him doing in your kids' lives, and if you have examples, mention how you see His touch in the life of your husband. Affirm, affirm, affirm. And let him hear the excitement you feel about watching God at work (but don't overdo it, or it may become monotonous and ineffective).

Tell him how much you need his help, how much his wisdom benefits you and your kids. Every man likes to feel needed. There's nothing a man appreciates more, whether he shows it quickly or not, than being asked by the woman he loves to be a help. Tell your husband you need his help for you to become everything God created you to be. Share your confidence that God put him in your life as a special blessing to help you reach the potential that He intended. Invite him to give you his ideas on how you can reach that goal, how you can attain your best.

Tell him you value his opinion. Find ways to encourage him by pointing out how much you also need his wise, helpful input and involvement in the lives of your kids. It may result in no more than a pattern of you and he taking turns reading a proverb on a regular basis with your kids, then supplying a simple but personal application on how you've seen that truth principle applied in everyday life.

But assure him that you need his participation and that you respect him for making the commitment and finding time to do it.

Tell him you really value and cherish his help in creating an atmosphere of discovery in your home where each family member can learn that God has a special plan for him or her, that He has invited each into a special relationship with Him, and that He has a unique mission and calling for each to help change the world. Assure your husband that the whole weight of this responsibility is not on his shoulders alone: you want, in every way possible, to share the responsibility with him of creating a home that honors God. Tell him your desire to have a home that regularly receives God's blessings, because the two of you are working together to build a family that pleases Him.

Ask him to pray with you and the kids. Tell your husband how much it would mean for him to pray *for you,* but assure him these don't need to be long, wordy prayers, just a sentence or two about a specific need you have. But then comes the most important part: as soon as you see an answer in response to your husband's prayer, *let him know.* Nothing helps make success more than experiencing success. There's something energizing and enticing about realizing that our prayers about something actually made a difference! So let him know that even in little things he's indeed making a difference.

Then it's a much easier step to pray with and for the kids—even brief prayers. And don't forget to share with him God's promise to answer. Jeremiah 33:3 is not only a great verse of Scripture but an absolute promise as well. Remember, God is far more ready to bless and answer our prayers than sometimes we are to offer them. If your husband has struggles praying for the kids while the whole family is together and everyone is listening, ask if he'll go with you into the room of each child after he or she has gone to sleep at night and pray then. Ask him to pray for one quality that God would put in that child's life and that He would supply a hedge of protection from dangers and discomforts they face daily.

Help him to find small successes. When your husband shows some spiritual leadership, even just a small amount, acknowledge and affirm it. If you want him to repeat even the little things you might see him do, tell him how well he did it. Remember, a journey of a thousand miles begins with a single step. We're all much more likely to get down the road a few miles if somebody affirms the first few steps!

Tell your husband how fortunate you feel that you're in this together. Let him know you're glad to be on his team. And by all means, pray for him daily and work at praying with him regularly.

Trust that the Holy Spirit is indeed at work both in your husband and in the lives of your kids.

To review, remember that a man's greatest fear is *inadequacy*. Counselors say that a woman's greatest fear is *insecurity*. Now I'll turn this over to Cheryl. Hopefully, husbands whose wives haven't bought in to your commitment to raise *on mission* children will find encouragement and insight.

Cheryl on Wives

Bob is right: insecurity drives many a woman to behave the way she does. In spite of all the progress we've made—earning as much money as many men (for those in the paid workforce), earning respect (if we stay home to raise our children)—a woman's role in today's society still leaves her with a certain amount of insecurity. I think that's one reason women tend to band together, forming relationships with one another and being supportive, whereas men are usually individualistic and competitive. We need each other.

The family I grew up in demonstrated to me the value of going to church and taking an active part. They had an admirable work ethic, much of which I attribute to their religious background, which emphasized responsibility. The fact that they were personally and professionally successful made me connect in my mind that regular church attendance must lead to character development. Certainly, that lesson had a lot of validity; being in church is a good thing, and we often grow in character as a result of faithful attendance. But through no particular fault of my parents, I was still missing a key point. It wasn't until I was in college that I found out the importance of having a personal *relationship* with Jesus over simply having a *religion*.

Elsewhere in this book I tell my story of how I learned from a college friend about committing myself to Jesus and inviting Him to reside in my heart. That moment, of course, changed everything . . . yet everything didn't change. And there's a big difference. That moment when I went back to my dorm room and prayed, I began a journey toward wholeness that I'm still experiencing today. In other words, my heart was immediately changed by the indwelling of the Holy Spirit, yet I had much to learn about living this new life as a follower of Christ.

For example, years later, after Bob and I married, I can remember one day when I was visiting a dear friend I've mentioned named Beverly Terrell. She was telling me about all these deep spiritual feelings she had and ways she applied them to raising her family. Frankly, I remember thinking, *What the heck is she talking about?* The truth is that Beverly was just more spiritually mature than I was. She had been walking with the Lord longer and had more wisdom. How I wish I'd admitted I needed her guidance! I'm sure she would have mentored me for all she was worth, and I would have grown in my relationship with Christ deeper and faster as a result.

I'm so encouraged when I see today's moms asking for help, calling on more mature women to guide them. As I grow older, I'm dedicating more of my time to being a life coach to younger women who have better sense than I did that day when I could have asked Beverly for more of her wisdom. You see, as a teen and college student, I didn't rebel in the sense that many in my generation rebelled. My challenges were more in the area of attitude. And there I was in the presence of a spiritual giant compared to myself, and I didn't have the humility to say, "I really don't know what you mean. Tell me more, more, more."

THOUGHTS THAT STYMIE PROGRESS

Here are additional thought processes I see in women that may keep them from coming on board with husbands who want homes that provide their kids a launching pad into the *on mission* lifestyle.

"I'm not qualified." I met a woman recently who told me she'd had a wild past. She felt inferior to other women, especially those Christians who seem to have it all together. She obviously had a great deal to learn about redemption, the lesson that Jesus had transformed her and washed away her unclean self. But she represents a lot of us who feel shame and don't think we're qualified to teach our children about God. She thought she had lost that right forever because of her rebelliousness as a young woman. Even women who are more at my end of that spectrum—we weren't behaviorally rebellious but our attitudes needed some adjusting (okay, a lot of adjusting)—sometimes think we're not qualified to give our children direction because we haven't been through what kids are confronted with today. God's message to all of us is "No, you're not qualified, but lean on Me, and I will show you the way."

Psalm 32:8 reminds us that "I [the Lord] will instruct you and teach you in the way you should go; / I will counsel you and watch over you." James 1:5 states, "If any of you lacks wisdom, he should ask God, who gives generously to all without finding fault, and it will be given to him." If you are the husband of a woman who doesn't think she's qualified to participate in the spiritual leadership you want your children to experience in their parents, encourage her to grow, to take risks, to mature in her knowledge of God's Word . . . but make clear to her that you won't be threatened by having a wife who grows stronger, or you will play into her insecurity of losing you. One of the most wonderful things Bob has done for me is to comment often how much he appreciates seeing me spend time in the Word and how much he values my wisdom with our kids.

"What's so hard about raising kids? I turned out okay!" Some wives think their husbands are overreacting by wanting to have devotionals or do activities to encourage their children to find God's plan for their lives. Frankly, these are moms who just don't get out enough! Sure, their parents may not have prevented them from seeing certain movies, but the world is different now—much different. In too many cases, kids confront dangerous ways of thinking and behaving just by going to school. They need to leave the house every day wearing the armor of God (Eph. 6:10–17), and they need to have the Word of God hidden in their hearts. A couple of hours with the church youth group are simply not enough support and preparation for facing the world today.

God's message to these moms is to trust in your husbands' wisdom and follow their leadership (Col. 3:18) in providing more spiritual guidance for your children than might have seemed necessary only a generation ago. If your wife has these attitudes, gently introduce her to the realities of what she hasn't yet learned about how the world operates, and assure her that you need her participation in making your home an *on mission* launching pad. Then make sure she understands that you won't resist or be threatened by her growth.

"I'm so tired." Today's women *are* tired! Even with all our technological advances, our families' lives are more hectic, even frantic, than at any time in the past. I often think what it must have been like for the pioneer women, pushing westward—without benefit of sunglasses! Seriously, they had hardships we can't even imagine enduring. And yet, while we may not be holding the reins on a team of horses pulling our covered wagons through muddy, deep-rutted trails, we do have incredible traffic to navigate . . . and soccer practice . . . and ringing telephones . . . and PTA meetings . . . and possibly even the demands of jobs outside our homes with bosses and employees, and—well, you get the picture.

My prayer is that these women will discover God's model for womanhood as Proverbs 31 describes. (Perhaps their priorities will even change, and they'll find their labors more directed at what's necessary and important.) And if you are a husband married to such a woman, recognize that she *is* tired and offer to help with her tasks, to lift her burden. Not only will you be getting her attention by tending to her very real needs, you will be modeling servant-leadership to her—and your kids. (*Servant-leadership* means following the example of Jesus: recognizing that a leader serves rather than being served.)

Also, you'll be providing her with another layer of security that you and she are a team, devoted *together* to raising Christ-following children. As her insecurities dwindle, she may discover she has the energy to be a full-fledged partner with you in their spiritual upbringing.

"I've blown it." Sometimes, for whatever reason, kids just don't seem spiritually responsive. A mom can feel ridiculous trying to keep bringing God into her kids' lives, especially if she suspects (because she's insecure) that she may have pushed them away. Here's an example where you, as a husband, need to teach her that you worship a God of second chances. Maybe you suspect she thinks she's blown it and this is why she's backed off from your family devotions or other efforts to teach about Christ. If so, you need to be more careful than ever to ask her for forgiveness, and you need to show forgiveness to her (not for the rebellious child whose attitude can be a result of so many factors in today's society, but for any transgressions between you). And then you need to let bygones be bygones—a hard part of forgiveness but essential, especially in a marriage. Forgiveness provides her with much-needed security.

Also, the process of forgiveness models coming back into the loving arms of God, calling Him "Abba" or "Daddy" (Rom. 8:15–17). And that's the atmosphere you want to create in your home: open arms for your spiritually unresponsive son or daughter eventually to climb back into, so you and your wife—together—can point them to the One who will guide them always, long after they've left the nest.

As we've said, it takes a lot of courage, as well as humility, to say and do what our spouses need, but we're convinced the effort is worth it. Although many strong Christians had only one parent as a role model, if you're *both* partnering as Mission Control, your home will have a far better chance of successfully launching your kids for life.

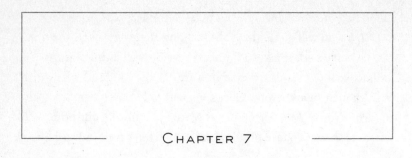

CHAPTER 7

MILESTONES
FOR A MEMORABLE,
MOTIVATIONAL JOURNEY

Dr. James Dobson has become America's quintessential parental adviser. His books have been runaway bestsellers. People flock when he speaks publicly. Millions tune in to his *Focus on the Family* radio program. And his fight for the family and its centrality in our society is becoming legendary.

Many of his findings are sobering for parents. In the book whose title says it all, *Parenting Isn't for Cowards,* Dobson relates how he asked radio listeners, "What are the greatest problems you face in dealing with your parents or in-laws, and how will you relate differently to your grown children than your parents related to you?" In the flood of answers, one challenge stood out: the inability or unwillingness of parents to let go of grown children and bless them in their own lives.

An incredible 44% of the letters received made reference to this failure of older adults to let go. It was as though some of the writers had
been waiting for years for that precise question to be asked . . . The
writers wanted desperately to be free, to be granted adult status, and
especially, to be respected by their parents. At the same time, they
were saying to them, "I still love you. I still need you. I still want you
as my friend. But I no longer need you as the authority in my life."[1]

All of us who are adults treasure having wings to soar into our
own adult lives. And we hope that our parents joyfully release us after
giving us roots. But as Dobson discovered, it doesn't happen enough.
Why?

Many parents miss the perspective that we are stewards of our
children, and we have them for only a short while. And our ultimate
goal is *not* to keep them but to raise them up, so we can joyfully and
confidently release them.

Gary Smalley and John Trent, other voices on successful family
life, say it well:

Many of you are familiar with the verse that tells you to "Train up
a child in the way he should go, and when he is old he will not
depart from it" (Proverbs 22:6). While the section referring to a
child's remembering his early training often gets top billing, it's
actually telling you to have a goal for the child's going! [Train him
up in the way he should go.] Getting your child ready to leave
home is a high calling.[2]

MARKING RITES OF PASSAGE

Again, why do some parents have trouble letting go so their kids can
take flight? And why are some kids unwilling to take off, even if parents
have prepared them for their missions and aren't holding them back?

Looking at several cultures helps us answer this question. We found that certain populations do a great job of marking and then celebrating milestones in a child's journey to adulthood. We believe this makes the mission both motivational and memorable.

Hispanic families sponsor a *Quinceanera* for girls turning fifteen. Jewish families celebrate the thirteenth birthday of a boy with a *bar mitzvah* and a *bat mitzvah* for girls turning twelve. Native Americans send their eleven- to thirteen-year-old adolescent boys on a journey called Vision Quest. Even NASA has a way of marking significant milestones in the mission of each spacecraft they launch. What these groups accomplish with their markers is to motivate by setting mission goals and to make the mission memorable, which reinforces the lessons learned.

As authors we can't think of any single event in the culture in which we were raised (Anglo and Protestant) that accomplishes this as thoughtfully as the cultures we researched. Events such as baptisms or affirmations of faith are significant, of course. But we as a family and others we interviewed have developed our own ways to mark rites of passage for our kids as they progress to adulthood. Later we'll share specific ideas you may want to incorporate into your family's life. And we hope to take this idea up a notch by calling the process "marking *guidestones*." You'll see more about this in the next pages. But first let's see what some cultures do to mark their rites of passage.

THE HISPANIC *QUINCEANERA*

When a Hispanic girl turns fifteen, she can participate in an experience called a *Quinceanera,* a milestone marker establishing that she is coming of age. While the customs and ceremonies vary between Hispanic countries and communities, they all embrace religious traditions, family virtues and values, as well as social responsibility.

It begins when her closest male friend escorts her down the aisle of her church for the festive event. Then comes a religious service with thanksgiving prayer, Bible reading, blessings from the parents, dedication of the young lady to God, and even renewal of baptismal vows with a special progressive candle-lighting ceremony. In some cultures, she cuts a ribbon barrier symbolizing her entrance into adulthood before God and the community.

A sponsor or family member presents her with fifteen roses— one for each year of her life—to signify her blossoming into woman-hood. She may carry a porcelain doll symbolizing her entrance into the church as a child. But during the ceremony, she exchanges the doll for other items—often in Catholic communities they use a rosary, a prayer book, or a Bible—representing her leaving behind her childish ways and taking up the Word of God and her responsi-bilities as a Christ-follower.

In some ceremonies she receives a tiara, denoting that she is a "princess" or daughter of the King. Her family may present her with a bracelet or ring to symbolize the unending circle of life and love into which she enters, plus the unending potential of her abilities and contributions; earrings as a reminder to listen to the Word of God and to respond to the needs of the world; and a cross, signify-ing the need for a stable faith in God and, out of that, faith in her-self and in her world.

The boys have been left out of the *Quinceanera*. But some moth-ers in Texas are starting to adapt a similar event and custom for their sons and are calling it a Beau Party.

THE JEWISH BAR MITZVAH AND BAT MITZVAH

At age thirteen the Jewish boy observes his bar mitzvah, and at twelve, the girl her bat mitzvah. Although these are relatively new celebra-tions, their origins date back to the midrash, an ancient tradition of Torah study to search out the fullness of what was spoken by the Divine Voice. They note the transition of a Jewish boy or girl moving from childhood into the realm of personal responsibility for his or her decisions. In fact, the Jewish father even prays, *"Baruch sage—petarani me-onsho shel zeh,"* meaning "Blessed is the One who has now freed me from responsibility for this one."[3] All those people who are meaningful to the Jewish son or daughter in his or her community of faith publicly and socially recognize the maturing child's moral and social responsibility.

THE NATIVE AMERICAN VISION QUEST

Between ages eleven and thirteen, a Native American boy experiences something broadly known as Vision Quest to help him begin to answer questions such as *Why am I here? What is my mission in life?* His preparation begins with a consultation with the community elders, who counsel the boy on the meaning of manhood, responsibility, leadership, and fulfilling his calling in life through dedication and hard work.

Then the boy fasts for five to ten days in a remote location such as a canyon, mountain, or desert. During these days he prays, seeking guidance and direction. He looks for answers in forms such as visions, dreams, signs, or inner convictions.

When he returns to the community, he shares his experiences with the elders, who probe the boy to help him interpret the vision and understand its meaning; then he shares it with the entire community. The leaders immediately begin a mentoring process to help the boy understand his role and function in the community, so he can start making an impact. The women and children translate the vision through music and art, perhaps weaving scenes of the vision into a tapestry or painting a mural. Through this medium the entire community participates in molding the boy so he can effectively fulfill his mission.

A significant aspect of Vision Quest is when the boy receives a name that represents his vision at a ceremony during which he officially enters manhood. Often, an accomplished member of the community who has carried a similar responsibility and function will be the one to present the boy with his name. After this, the newly named man leaves behind his adolescence and assumes his place in the community.

If You Want to Know About Launches, Go to the Experts

Fall! There's nothing like it, especially if you were raised in Michigan and Indiana (as we were). For us, fall always meant football. The smell of burning leaves. Cozy fires crackling. Sweaters coming out from their hiding places. Apple cider and hayrides.

But *that* fall was different. We had just moved to Florida. And leaves don't turn gold and crimson there, let alone blanket the ground with their glorious autumn colors.

So there we were, walking our second-grade son up to his new school in a Tampa suburb. And although the season was fall, we were dripping with sweat. But the climate was just one of our family's adjustments to a metropolitan beach community. And on that day Bryan wondered what challenges lay across his path as he ventured into the unknown space of new friends, unexpected competitors, and the dreaded pecking order.

We had just reached the steps of Bryan's school when suddenly everyone's head swiveled to the eastern sky. What in the world were they looking at? Why were they glued to the horizon? Was it a strange Florida custom we hadn't learned yet?

That's when our second grader pointed and shouted, "It's the shuttle!"

Sure enough, flames followed by the plume of smoke streaking across Florida's crystal-clear sky reminded us of a news broadcast announcing that day as another incredible launch of astronauts aboard the space shuttle. They were off on their latest mission. We joined the others with our mouths hanging open in amazement.

DESIGNED TO FLY ON THEIR OWN

In our family we recall that as the day we were struck for the first time with the similarity of America's space program to our job as parents. We pray for our kids and prepare them and train them, all in an effort to *launch* them on their lives' journeys. And as with the shuttle, there may be multiple launches, with a few false starts and even times when the shuttle is called back to Earth before going into orbit. But ultimately, our kids are designed to fly on their own. As Christ-following parents, we want them to do it successfully to complete their lives' missions.

Another way of saying it is this: *We give them roots to give them wings. We give them a launching pad so they can take flight.* And as anyone who has followed the history of the space program knows, the result can be success . . . or tragedy. Consider what we learned from some NASA astronauts:

- Launches can't happen on just any old day. Conditions must be conducive, and the odds need to be highly in favor of success, because there's far too much at stake to rely on chance. (And if that's true with a shuttle, think about our kids!)
- Once the "Go" is given, things begin to move fast but in an orderly and predetermined sequence. Solid-rocket-booster separation occurs two minutes into the flight. They've served their purpose and would be excess baggage from there on out, even making further progress untenable (like going to school without that well-loved teddy bear). As with all journeys, not everything is needed at every stage of the trip, and the boosters are left behind.
- Ironically, the orbiter flies upside down during the ascent phase of leaving the pad. (Sounds like some of our kids, doesn't it!)

- The external tank is jettisoned (you know, sort of like cutting Mom's apron strings). It has served its purpose of providing 526,000 gallons of fuel necessary to blast out of the earth's gravitational force.

- Once in flight, the crew closely monitors main engine performance, eventually throttling back and shutting down. Now the launch is successful and the mission under way. (We parents need to help our kids know when to fire the engines and when to throttle back, don't we?)

- For success, every flight's mission depends on the calling, training, and work of the flight crew and Mission Control. Each astronaut brings to the mission a unique set of skills, knowledge, strengths, and gifts but remains dependent on the others for success. No one is an island in this journey. The crew can accomplish far more by cooperating than can be achieved by the sum of each person's individual efforts. (Sort of reminds you of life, doesn't it?)

- Mission Control oversees and gives general direction to the flight, with responsibility for support, guidance, resources, and counsel to ensure success in the mission—and to act swiftly in response to any emergency. Failure is not an option! (Sound familiar?)

- The ground crew complements the efforts of Mission Control, giving help when necessary. (What parent doesn't need a ground crew of grandparents, teachers, coaches, church staff, or friends of the family who love the kids and want them to succeed?)

- As we've mentioned, in flight the astronauts have the freedom to override what Mission Control instructs if they decide they have better information about their conditions than Houston. (Like kids—and adults—they have free will.) The wise crew listens to the counsel of Mission Control, which is made up of aerospace experts committed to the mission and astronauts who have flown before.

HOUSTON, WE HAVE A PROBLEM

Every astronaut lives with the reality that circumstances can mandate an emergency with no alternative but to abort. And while aborts are unwanted, they are sometimes necessary. The goal is not to point fingers but to get the crew back safely to launch another day. Once that's accomplished, they debrief with questions such as these:

What did we learn?
What needs to be improved or changed?
What did we do right?
What was avoidable, and what was not?
What will bring success the next time?

These are good questions for us as parents too, don't you agree? There are times when, with the best of intentions, we launch our kids into a new adventure, a new direction, or a new opportunity, and it just doesn't go right. Warning systems start to flash. Alarms begin to sound. And quick adjustments have to be made. For example:

Our son won't talk about his friends or bring them to the house.
Our daughter's grades plummet.
Our son answers our question with a question (avoiding our question!).
Our daughter begins dressing provocatively.
Our son has enormous mood swings.

All of us who step into the scary world of parenting must remember there is no shame in changing courses (what we call "making a course correction"). It may be the very action that allows our child to fly another day. The shame comes from being unwilling to step in as Mission Control and help the flight get back for a safe landing, regrouping, and preparation for a successful relaunch.

Maybe you allowed your daughter to join an organization with a name that sounded fine, even spiritual. But now she's moody and dressing weird and listening to strange music—and arriving home with dilated pupils. Maybe your son went to a school where he thought he could study, but too many distractions and tailgate parties are getting in the way. He just can't seem to handle it. A year at home, attending community college, might be just the answer.

We learned from the astronauts who so generously gave of their time and expertise that the most critical point of a shuttle mission is ignition. If everyone in Mission Control and the ground crew has done his or her job right, the shuttle launches in a blaze of glory. But if someone became distracted or didn't watch carefully enough, things can go awry in a hurry. The result can be a thrust vector off by only a degree or two at ignition. One of three possibilities may occur:

1. The shuttle is so far off course and out of control that it must be destroyed.

2. Less catastrophic but still tragic, the shuttle is so far off course that the trajectory is altered, causing it to wind up in the wrong orbit. While the astronauts aboard may survive, they don't realize the full potential for their mission.

3. The entire mission is aborted and the shuttle is brought back to Earth until it can be relaunched at a later date.

IT'S THE LITTLE THINGS THAT COUNT

We've described how the 1986 *Challenger* tragedy brought a halt to the space shuttle program for thirty-two months. Seven brave astronauts lost their lives shortly after launch as the explosion was captured on video and replayed many times on television.

The problem sounded insignificant: a faulty O-ring on one of *Challenger's* twin solid rockets. The O-ring did not seal properly, allowing hot gases to burst through and rupture seals and joints, leading to the tragic explosion.

And so it is with life and the launch of our kids. It's usually not the *big* things that bring them down. It's the little ones that parents ignore. And sometimes the parents don't have all the facts to make a decision whether to support the launch or abort the mission. Many times as parents we're working with our gut instincts . . . a sense of foreboding . . . an innate ability to see beyond what everybody else is doing and realize a tragic outcome. Maybe we went through something similar as kids ourselves. Maybe our parents didn't diagnose the problem, and we learned a very tough lesson the hard way. However we recognize the need to abort the mission, ultimately it comes down to our having the guts to make judgment calls, regardless of the criticism and hurt feelings that may result.

MAKING THE MOST OF THE MILESTONES

In the American space program, every crew has tasks to accomplish and milestones to reach: payloads to deploy, repairs to make. Maybe the mission is to enhance a space station, retrieve a satellite, or conduct a scientific experiment.

At NASA every accomplishment is celebrated. And not just by one astronaut who may have accomplished a feat, but by the whole team: Mission Control, the ground crew, everyone who played a part. Time and work demands may limit the size of the celebration, but NASA has learned the importance of marking significant accomplishments, both in the air and back on the ground. Marking these milestones is critical for the emotional well-being of the team. NASA knows that demands of performance without celebrations of accomplishment create angry and edgy crew members.

The astronauts will remember these accomplishments for a lifetime. The milestones of a mission are etched into their memory banks. The celebrations are a cherished tradition, serving as encouragement for future challenges, boosters for hurdles in the journey ahead. Milestone markers bring satisfaction, and they offer hope for greater tomorrows. They say, *Mission accomplished!* But the total journey is by no means over. The genius of the space shuttle is that it was built to fly again and again.

What insight for us as parents. It's so important to create milestone celebrations in the lives of our children as they chart their journey. One thing we've learned is this: our kids cherish experiences far more than things. Objects break, become old hat, out of style, and boring. But experiences live forever because they live in the heart and mind.

Most important, celebrating milestones with our kids helps them prioritize what is truly important in life. It gives them memories to bank for the mission ahead. And it provides a bond between parent and child as they celebrate the significance of life's journey and mission *together*.

How are you doing in capturing the milestones of life with your kids? If you're interested in ideas in this realm of successful missions, hang on and keep reading. We've got some thought provokers for you!

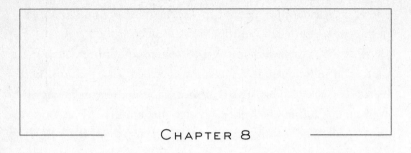

CHAPTER 8

MILESTONES? BETTER YET, GUIDESTONES

Webster's Dictionary defines *milestone* as "a stone serving as a mile-post, or a significant point in development."

But could there be a better and more appropriate term? Try on *guidestone*. The *Oxford Dictionary* defines a guidestone as . . .

- A marker used to point direction

- A marker used to determine distance

- A marker to warn of dangers

How appropriate! Special events built into the lives of our kids can do any combination of the above or all three. As a parent who loves your children and wants the best for them, you can build into their lives several ideas we are proposing as *guidestones*. These can help your children as they move toward a future that fulfills the eight principles we share in this book.

You may want to do one, two, or more of the ideas. Or they may spark your creativity to think of ideas for *guidestones* in your child's life that we don't mention here but that would be tailor-made for you, your family, and your child or teen. Meanwhile, here are a few we and our friends recommend.

JOURNAL OF THE JOURNEY

Scrapbooking is a rage sweeping across North America. A recent conference in this exploding trend was held near our home, and it drew thirty thousand women. Scrapbooking is all about making records of significant life events and experiences and putting them into a format that makes a wonderful gift to keep for a lifetime.

Have you ever thought of putting together a journal to give to your children when they leave home or marry? If so, the best time to start is when they arrive in your family. We weren't quite so bright. Now we're putting together a journal for each of our three kids as Christmas gifts, but we waited until they were in their twenties to begin.

Not so with our friends Debi and David Doverspike. After they married, they waited ten years for kids. One reason was David's worry that kids might be a real challenge and difficulty; he thought life as a married couple without children would be less complicated.

But from the moment he saw his first child born, David has been convinced that God has a very special plan for each one of them. The Doverspikes decided that as each child turned ten, the parents would share a special event with him or her. It might be a two-week trip to a place the child wanted to visit. Darcy, now sixteen, and Rachel, ten, both chose England. Ricky, now fourteen, chose Hawaii. During the trip, the parents poured out quality and quantity time, and they carried out Deuteronomy 6, which talks about teaching the principles of God's ways and will as we rise up, walk through the day, and lay down at night. The challenge was to present this sort of information to the child during his or her trip in normal conversations while sightseeing. These trips helped the Doverspikes to bond with their kids as well as to share, through everyday discussions, many foundational principles the parents feel are important to pass along to the next generation.

Throughout the process, David has been keeping journals, one for each child. (That's right, we said *David*. Although wives usually do this, we want you to know that husbands can do it very well too!) He's recording special events, memories from the trips, admirable qualities he notices the child is developing, and even his prayers and hopes for that child. He and Debi plan to give the journals to each of their kids on the day each gets married.

What a powerful idea! It captivated our imaginations and helped put us into action. So we've been making a list of things we plan to include in the journals we're doing for our kids, and we share them here with you.

We recommend that you purchase a nice leather-bound journal from a business store and start your own. Perhaps you'll use one color of ink for the lead-ins and another color to complete your personalized thoughts, insights, and memories for your kids. We list suggested lead-ins here and invite you to keep in touch with us by visiting totallifeimpact.com for more ideas.

- We waited _____ years for God to bring you into our home.
- We knew God was preparing us for your arrival. One special way He did this was . . .
- Your entry into our lives was marked by . . .
- The time and place of your arrival were . . .
- The reason we chose your name was . . .

- The earliest and most memorable character traits we noticed in you were . . .

- You brought us so much joy and laughter. One of our funniest memories of you is . . .

- Our prayerful hopes for God's plan and future for you were . . .

- God has a special call on your life. Here's one memory of how we began to see that and realized how His hand is on you . . .

- The Bible is God's Owner's Manual. A few of the ways it has influenced our lives as your parents are . . .

- Two biblical concepts we've tried to instill in your life are . . .

Trust us, the older they get the more they'll love, appreciate, and value your effort!

CELEBRATING FOUNDATIONAL *GUIDESTONES* OF DIFFERENT FAITH TRADITIONS

We happen to be Southern Baptists, and one of the highlights of life's journey, we believe, is the ordinance of believer's baptism. We refer to it as an "ordinance" because we feel it's a symbolic picture of an internal reality. A wedding band externally and visibly symbolizes the love a man and a woman have for each other and the commitment they've made. Likewise, we believe baptism by immersion is the external picture of the internal reality of surrendering one's life to Christ by an act of our own will and aligning with Christ to fulfill His mission through us to change the world.

But it never ceases to amaze us how people in far too many evangelical churches place relatively little emphasis and celebration on the event. It's not that they don't consider it important or that the congregation and family don't make baptism special. The issue is that it's often over in about five minutes, and little goes on afterward to mark it as a spiritual *guidestone* in the children's lives.

Cheryl grew up in the Lutheran church. There (as in other denominations) an event called *confirmation* is a very significant occurrence in a young person's spiritual journey. After weeks of study and spiritually related experiences, a celebration service publicly acknowledges each member of the class as having reached his or her point of confirmation, a valued step on the path toward spiritual maturity and responsibility.

We personally hold the view that baptism following a personal decision to follow Christ represents the best biblical model, yet we find it inspiring to listen to the things the kids who have gone through confirmation classes have learned. Frankly, we've observed that many of them become more intellectually aware of the basis and basics of their faith than some kids in evangelical traditions because of the intensely focused time of learning and memorizing.

Regardless of the denomination or tradition, many parents we've talked to expressed a desire to make events such as believer's baptism or affirmation of faith at confirmation into motivational, memorable points in their kids' journeys to adulthood. But often they added that they didn't know how. Here are some ideas to stimulate your thinking as you consider how to do this for your children or grandchildren.

First, talk with your child about the upcoming event and how it is special to your family. Share your anticipation and excitement and why you feel it's so important. Invite the child to tell why he or she feels it's important. Ask the child what thoughts are going through his or her mind. Be sure to allow your children or grandchildren to make comments in their own words, rather than giving them questions they can respond to with a simple yes or no. It's essential for the children to articulate their processes.

Second, as the big day approaches, be ready to make a movie of the event. With today's affordable digital cameras, it would be a shame for any parent not to record such a special occasion. And don't just film the event. Do some on-camera interviews. Ask your child to express in his or her own words how and why the event is significant. Ask family members and friends of your child to reflect on the occasion. The point is to create a record of the child's thoughts and feelings at the time of the event and the encouragement others offered in the child's life.

Third, have a special certificate made for the one being honored through believer's baptism or affirmation of faith at confirmation. Don't settle for a black-and-white certificate. Find one that's colorful and looks beautiful when framed—every bit as nice as a certificate awarded to a sports team at the end of a season. If you, as a parent or grandparent, would like one to award to your child or grandchild, we invite you to go on-line to totallifeimpact.com, where we offer, for free, both baptism and affirmation (confirmation) certificates to mark these *guidestone* moments. You can download them and fill them out yourself, or have someone letter them for you using calligraphy. Have them framed, and present them to your children. It's our gift to you!

Fourth, host a special celebration meal with family and friends after the event. Acknowledge the child or grandchild as the honoree, again emphasizing the importance of this spiritual *guidestone*. Be sure to include a time of prayer and dedication of the young person plus a prayer of blessing and protection over his or her life.

Fifth, make plans now to recognize annually the significance of this special occasion. Think of this: every year we celebrate the passage of birthdays when all we're doing is becoming one year older. But rarely do we celebrate the annual marker of such an important spiritual high point as baptism or affirmation (confirmation). Go out of your way to

- Buy a special card and send it to your child on that date every year to remind him or her of the importance of this spiritual *guidestone.*

- Every few years, write a letter telling your child the character qualities and talents you see developing in his or her life as an affirmation of the spiritual growth taking place.

- Give a prayer of thanksgiving on the anniversary of the special event to highlight the ongoing value of reaching this *guidestone.*

Remember Beth and Steve Puckett from the beginning of this book? (How could you forget—you were an imaginary guest of this family!) The Pucketts grasped this opportunity. When their children came to know Christ as personal Savior by an act of faith and a decision of choice, the parents hosted a luncheon following the baptism.

Beth had been intrigued by a children's evangelism resource called the Wordless Book. It's a delightful resource that uses colors to explain the plan of salvation and what it means to know Jesus Christ as Savior. Using a Wordless Book with colored pages, any individual, including a young person, can effectively share the significant points of a biblical plan of salvation with kids.

As we mentioned, Beth purchased balloons in each of the colors found in the Wordless Book. At a certain point in the luncheon, she asked her child, who had been baptized that day, to share the plan of salvation using the colored balloons as illustrations for the different biblical points of the gospel. The impact on their kids' friends was tremendous!

Making these events special, as well as memorable and motivational, takes a little time and creativity—but the payback is forever! (By the way, if you want to use the Wordless Book, a product of Child Evangelism Fellowship, find out more information at www.cefonline.com.)

Stepping into the Teens

We've discussed cultures with effective rites of passage to celebrate the movement into the key teen years and toward the maturity and responsibility of adulthood. Perhaps the best known are the bar mitzvah and bat mitzvah for young men and women in the Jewish culture. For their exemplary family-centered and faith-based commitment to such celebrations, we owe our Jewish friends a great deal. But we wonder why such a celebration couldn't happen in the Christian culture. Others have written books on the subject, one of the best of which is *Spiritual Milestones* by Jim and Janet Weidmann and Otis and Gail Ledbetter. There you'll find an extremely detailed process. But our desire here is to whet your appetite and give you a vision for what such a celebration could be. We'll start by telling you about the Overtons.

Nat and Victoria were members of our church when we had the joy of pastoring at the wonderful First Baptist Church of Norfolk, Virginia. Along with their son, Jonathan, and daughter, Crystal, Nat and Victoria quickly became friends and encouraging supporters. As an African-American family, they brought a great richness and diversity to the congregation and helped add a significant number of African-American and ethnic families to the church makeup.

One day we received the devastating news that Nat had cancer. In no time he began to spiral downhill. With a teenage daughter and young son depending on him, things couldn't have been worse. But you never would have known it to visit Nat—or, for that matter, Victoria. They were the picture of faith in action when we dropped by to see Nat, hoping to bring him encouragement and build up his spirits. But one day, it was Bob who had his spirits lifted.

When Nat inquired where Bob was heading and what he would be doing, Nat promised that he would be praying for Bob during the time frame in which he would be speaking in Atlanta. Little did Bob know that during that very time period, Nat would step from Earth into eternity, having faithfully remembered to lift up his pastor to the Lord Jesus Christ, whom he was about to meet. Victoria told us that Nat's prayer for Bob was the last thing he said before dying.

Though Nat's death was a great loss to the family, Victoria has marched forward with amazing strength in the years since. Recently she celebrated a rite of passage for Jonathan as he came into his teen years, establishing a *guidestone* on which he could look back for the rest of his life.

It was quite an accomplishment for a single mom, but Victoria's own parents wisely built within her a character that overcomes difficulties. When she was a teen, her dad was a pastor and the family had moved to a new church. Kids in the school weren't exactly sensitive to integration—the school was 95 percent white. Victoria says, "I felt lost and trapped. I found that a lot of the people I met during that time did not like the color of my skin. They made comments about it. I told my parents that I didn't think these people liked me, and I wanted to go back where we'd come from.

"But my parents said, 'Maybe this is God's plan for you. Let's try it for one year, and if you still don't like it, we'll go back to the old school.'" Victoria tried to relax, but her situation went downhill, culminating with some white students trying to stuff her in a locker. Taunting her, they declared she wasn't worth the time of day and should be home taking care of the laundry—implying that since she was black, she was good only for cleaning.

Angry, Victoria hurried home and told her father what had happened. She demanded a change immediately. "We can do that," he responded thoughtfully. "That's not an insurmountable problem. However, if God wants to use you mightily, He might have you in a situation where you have to change those people's hearts. He might be using you to do that."

"Does that mean I have to return to school?" Victoria shot back.

"You ought to try," her father counseled. "But I'm going to leave that up to you and what you think God would have you do."

After spending a lot of time in prayer—and dread—Victoria went back to school the next day. To her amazement, she discovered a new set of friends: students who had been waiting for someone to stand up, to be a valiant warrior, to provide some leadership. But the most satisfying experience came near the end of the school year, when one of the boys who had stuffed her into the locker approached her. "Victoria, I've watched you all year, and I realize I was wrong. Please forgive me."

Because of that, Victoria came to the life-changing conclusion that "I wasn't going to please a lot of people just because of who I was, but I could make the decision not to follow their way of life or attitudes. I chose to follow the way of life that God set down for me, and by doing that, I committed to help others overcome their obstacles."

Victoria has continued to overcome one obstacle after another. As a mother, she wanted to pass along this overcoming legacy to her children. When Jonathan reached age thirteen, Victoria put together a rite-of-passage ceremony to which she invited a number of people who meant a lot in Jonathan's life. She even went to the effort to have a video message from Bob to Jonathan, telling him how privileged he was to have had Nat for a dad, how much Nat loved the Lord and Jonathan, and how much Jonathan would want to honor Nat by loving the Savior Nat had loved. This message is in harmony with Victoria's own message to Jonathan every time he says, "I would love to live up to my dad and who he was." That's when Victoria always responds with this challenge: "I would love for you to live up to *Christ,* because Christ is the One your dad followed and tried to live for." Smart mom!

So as the big ceremony approached, Victoria planned the guest list:

- Victoria's brother, Samuel Jones, who is a deacon in his own church and took Jonathan under his wing when his father died

- Mike and Jeanine Molzahn, whose son, Richard, had grown up with Jonathan, been in Scouts with Jonathan, and gone through homeschooling with Jonathan. With Richard being white and Jonathan black, Victoria calls them "the perfect salt-and-pepper brothers."

- Bob Boiler, who was Jonathan's scoutmaster

- John, Jonathan's pastor at the time, and his wife, Connie

- Bob Reccord (by video)—their former pastor and family friend

The night of the celebration included a wonderful dinner followed by an opportunity to honor and challenge Jonathan. Samuel spoke on family heritage and the roots from which Jonathan had come; he said the future of those roots depended on Jonathan continuing to live the qualities that had been so important to his dad and still were to his mom.

Mike and Jeanine spoke on how a friend sticks closer than a brother regardless of race, circumstances, pressures, or expectations. They honored Jonathan for being such a great friend to their son and for the contribution Jonathan had been to their family.

Scoutmaster Boiler reminded Jonathan of the Boy Scout pledge and qualities he had promised to uphold, such as being courteous, being a man of honor, exhibiting strength, and being a man of integrity. He said that just as he had enjoyed the privilege of being a scoutmaster to Jonathan, there was a Master much more significant to whom Jonathan was accountable, and His name was Jesus Christ.

John and Connie Powers talked to him about being a minister and having a servant's heart. John later had the privilege of praying for Jonathan and his future.

And Victoria, his mom, reminded Jonathan that she had been almost forty-one years old when he was born. She reveled in the fact that even late surprises can be amazing blessings—and Jonathan had been exactly that. All of the people present challenged Jonathan to walk in honor of his dad, but in the footprints of Jesus Christ, whom his dad loved deeply.

Toward the end of the ceremony, Jonathan was presented with a purity ring signifying the challenge to commit to sexual purity until the day he was married. Victoria reminded him that the ring in its circular form had neither a beginning nor an ending—just as God's love for him was unending. She challenged him to be able to stand one day in the front of a church with friends and family looking on, presenting himself as a pure vessel to the young lady he would be marrying, whoever she is and wherever she might be today.

Victoria and the others challenged him to keep a clean mind as a way to keep himself pure, because sex begins in the mind. They shared Psalm 119:9 with Jonathan to challenge him to step up to the responsibility and accountability of becoming a young man not far from the seemingly elusive goal of becoming an adult.

And what kind of difference did that ceremony make in Jonathan's life? It's paying off in big dividends. Not long ago, Jonathan was chosen by some kids as their "practice dummy" for fights. When Victoria inquired what the fighting was about, he told her that some guys had decided to pick him out as the one to hassle on a regular basis. She looked Jonathan straight in the eye and said: "The next time somebody corners you, tell them that the Lord says not to lay a hand quickly on any man, and that you, even as a Christian, *do* have the right to defend yourself." (See Gen. 14:20.)

Jonathan did exactly what his mom suggested. At the time, she wasn't even sure her son was listening. But when Jonathan confronted his tormentors, he added a few words of his own: "God loves you and has a plan for you!"

The boy who was hassling Jonathan sneered, "What kind of plan can God have for me? I'm not even sure God knows kids like me exist."

The boy's father had left, and his mother was working long

hours to make ends meet. The boy wanted to prove he was "a man," so he took the challenge from his gang of peers to take out Jonathan— the guy they called "that little Christian."

Jonathan turned the tables on the boy when he answered, "I understand what you're saying. My dad died when I was young, and all I have is my mom. But she's told me violence isn't the way to solve anything. She told me I have a friend who's with me wherever I go, and His name is Christ."

The door to the heart of Jonathan's young adversary swung open, and Jonathan shared how he came to know Christ and how the young man could as well. To everybody's astonishment, the boy ended up becoming a Christian, and now he and Jonathan are best buddies!

So if you wonder whether a spiritual foundation and the acknowledgment of spiritual priorities can make a difference in the lives of your kids, remember Jonathan!

CELEBRATING THE RETURNING PRODIGAL

If you're a parent with a child who went through the prodigal stage, you know the heartbreak, the gut-gnawing fear, the deep and abiding sense of failure, as well as the desire to experience a glimmer of hope—regardless.

One of the Bible's best-known texts is Luke 15. It contains the stories of three lost treasured possessions: a sheep (which the shepherds called by name in those days), a wedding coin (like a wedding ring today), and a beloved son.

Parents with prodigal children are desperate to know "Is there hope?" They also wonder, *What will I do if my prodigal child comes home?*

We share our friend Tim's words of how he established a *guidestone* event for a prodigal son that launched everyone involved into a hopeful future.

In raising our children, my wife and I tried—like other Christian parents—to provide godly guidance and instruction. Sometimes we were successful, but many times we fell short, a story we've heard from many parents. While we had some control over the home environment, we had absolutely none in school.

Fortunately, our school system had a strong program called Say No to Drugs. From first through twelfth grades, this message was taught, and we reinforced it at home. This was also significant to me in a professional way, because I was in the substance-abuse services industry.

When we discussed drug abuse, my children nodded their heads and said they understood. To reinforce their compliance, one of my children said he was the designated safe driver and all the parents depended on him—just in case. I was so proud of him and trusted him implicitly! In school, he was a serious student with good grades, never once earning a misconduct report.

When he graduated from high school, I shared with other parents how fortunate we were that we "dodged a bullet." He'd been accepted at a conservative Christian college, and when my wife and I returned home after driving him to college on August 24, 2001, we were at total peace. My son was in a safe place!

On September 11 the World Trade Center collapsed.

On September 24 our world collapsed! My son called and said he was in jail on drug possession charges. He had a sense of humor, so I thought he was joking, and I laughed. But he screamed at me over the phone: "I'm in jail, Dad!"

I was numb. A cold, gripping fear descended over me.

The next morning I visited him, praying that the Holy Spirit would guide me. How was I going to react when I saw him? I felt like hitting him! But God's grace descended on me, and I was able to be calm and caring, even though I was in turmoil on the inside.

Expecting the worst, he had a defiant look on his face when he saw me. I surprised him by hugging him and saying I would help him through this trial. It was not the reaction he expected after eighteen years of hearing about the dangers of drugs.

Over the next year, we painstakingly—together and individually—worked through the issues, and there were many. For him and for me. We learned a lot about ourselves and about each other. Each time we were at a crossroad, God provided an answer. Many godly people entered our lives at just the right moment, providing exactly the right guidance. There were prayers and tears too many to count.

During this time of inner healing for both of us, I read a book by Henri Nouwen entitled *The Return of the Prodigal Son*. It had a profound impact on me, because the author provides help not only for the prodigal but also for the father and the older son. It helped me put our lives in perspective. I read about grief, compassion, unconditional love, forgiveness, and generosity—all emotions that I would experience deeply firsthand.

When my son turned twenty-one, my wife suggested we do something special, recognizing that he had matured into a responsible and caring individual. Years earlier I had purchased a very ancient Roman ring—probably two thousand years old—depicting a warrior riding in a chariot. As I looked at it, it reminded me that my son was a warrior, persevering through battles of doubt, self-esteem, and anxiety. He had proven to be a fighter, an overcomer. And I was very proud of him!

And if the truth be known, I would have gone through the pain again to be able to receive the blessings that resulted from our trial.

So on his twenty-first birthday, I gave my son a card that read:

Dear T.J.,

Your mom and I are very proud of you. On your twenty-first birthday, I am giving you one of my ancient rings. This ring represents the strength and courage you've shown as you persevered through difficult times. The chariot warrior symbolizes your Spartan heritage. In the face of difficulties, you *never* gave up. You succeeded with your head held high. May you always pursue your dream. You have a great future!

Love, Dad

If you've had a child who's walked the road of the prodigal, remember that Luke 15 is not so much about a rebellious child as it is about a loving, forgiving, and supporting parent: the Father. Maybe God is giving you a chance as a parent to show the qualities that only He can give when things are less than ideal. But it could be that in those very qualities your child will see God in a fresh and unexpected way, as he's never seen Him before—and where he least expected to see Him.

And remember that the real truth of Luke 15 is that there's not just one prodigal, but two. You don't have to run away from home to be a prodigal. One son showed outward rebellion, the other passive-aggressive resistance. One turned around, and one, though at home, stayed far removed.

When a child comes home, whatever you do, don't miss the opportunity to celebrate with a *guidestone* moment how far he's come, where he is today, plus a gentle reminder of where he doesn't want to go again.

In the next chapter we'll tell you what we do in our family to celebrate *guidestones* and how you can use our ceremony.

CHAPTER 9

CELEBRATING YOUR CHILD'S WINGS

Celebrating *guidestone moments* and *guidestone events* should never be complicated but rather should fit into the normal lifestyles and traffic patterns in a family's life. One of those inevitable moments is when our kids, after reaching young adulthood, finally launch out and leave home. For some it happens as they enter college. For others it's when they head into the military. Still others who stayed home for college years may launch into a job or marriage that finally takes them away from home base.

Celebrating such an event is a wonderful opportunity to endorse and support their stepping out of the nest and flying on their own wings. After all, by that point we've given all the roots we can give, and now we must just as readily and joyfully be ready to give them wings.

It's also at this point in life especially that we move from being primarily parent and overseer to being friend and adviser—when requested. It's a change in roles for both child and parent.

A New Kind of Family Crest

One joy we had was finding a creative way to celebrate the launching from home of our two daughters and our son. Not knowing quite what to do and not finding anything in the marketplace to help us, we created our own *guidestone marker* to aid in making the event significant. We decided to present our children with a distinguished wall hanging shaped like a crest with symbols representing biblical principles that guide our family. Where did we get our inspiration for the design? In Europe, where we have always been enamored with the family crests in that culture. Often the crest includes a shield divided into quadrants with qualities illustrated in each that represent values the family or clan held dear. So we thought, *Why not create a crest for our family?*

Bob found an illustrator who drew up a family crest consisting of a shield with four quadrants. We then discussed what qualities we hoped to see reflected in our children as they launch into their adult lives. We agreed on four that the artist helped us illustrate. We want our children to be

1. Biblically grounded—depicted by the Ten Commandments tablets (Old Testament) and an unfolding scroll (New Testament)

2. Holy Spirit–guided—depicted by a descending dove

3. Servant-hearted—depicted by a basin, towel, and sandals representing Christ washing His disciples' feet

4. *On mission*–focused—depicted by a bowl of salt and a New Testament oil lamp with a flame representing the call to be salt and light wherever we go

We then took the artwork to a trophy shop, where it was mounted on a plaque and covered with Plexiglas for presentation.

Bryan was the first for whom we did this. We surprised him with a dinner attended by people who had meant a lot in his life and had contributed a great deal to the success he had become. We invited several guests to give Bryan a challenge based on one of the biblical qualities in the crest's quadrants.

- His former student pastor had remained in Bryan's life even as he grew beyond his teen years. He challenged him to be salt and light wherever God took him in his journey.
- A good friend had invested a lot of love and time in Bryan's growth into manhood. We invited this man, an attorney, to challenge Bryan to treat the Word of God as the most significant book he would ever have in his life— which it would be only if he read, applied, and obeyed it.
- The man who would become Bryan's father-in-law challenged him on nurturing a servant-hearted attitude in his leadership, wherever his work and life placed him. He focused on the truth that true leaders—great leaders—are always servant-leaders.
- As his parents, we took the fourth quadrant. We challenged our son to be Spirit-directed, always depending on the Holy Spirit and His role in his life (as depicted in John 14–16) to be his internal guidance system, as well as his warning system.

Bryan's younger sister, Ashley, happened to be in town the night we hosted this special event, and she spoke from her heart as sister to brother. This ended up being one of the most emotional points of the evening. It's amazing how deep into their hearts siblings will reach at times like this, as they become older and wiser.

We then gathered around Bryan and placed our hands on him, each giving a charge based on the qualities each of us had addressed, each praying over him God's richest blessings for both the present and the future. We then awarded him the plaque with the crest. At the bottom of the plaque was a verse we chose specially for him.

We held the same ceremony for each of our girls; we kept the crest the same, but we changed the verses.

This was how we chose as parents to officially launch them into adulthood as they left home. They departed knowing that they went with our blessing, our prayers, our support, and our encouragement. We were communicating that we would always be ready to stand with them and support them, but we also would-strive as best we could never to get in their way or be hovering parents, failing to recognize their adulthood status.

If you've been looking for a way to hold a *guidestone celebration* and need some tools to help you do it, we've tried to make it easy for you. We invite you to go on-line at totallifeimpact.com, then click on an icon that says Launching Your Kids for Life. It will link you to a Web page where you will find at least twelve biblically based characteristics that you can choose to put on the quadrants of your own family crest. We've also included approximately seventy Scripture verses that you can use, as we did with our children, to put at the bottom of the plaque as a Commissioning Life Verse tailored for your child. You can then order the plaque on-line, and it will be custom-crafted and mailed to you for the special event.

By the way, you may wonder if we've had any results from these commissioning services. One of our greatest joys came from our oldest daughter, Christy. When we did the commissioning for her, she had moved to San Antonio for a new direction in her work life. The challenge was that she wasn't finding any good friends to spend time with, and she was working incredibly long hours. So even if she did find friends, she didn't have much time to spend with them.

On the night of her commissioning, we asked her what was the most important challenge in her life that we could pray about. With a sad expression, she said she wished she had some friends in San Antonio. That request became the focus of our prayer for her. It was incredible when, much later, in normal passing conversation she brought up out of the blue: "By the way, do you remember when you prayed for me to make some friends? A few months later I happened to stop and take stock of my life. I realized that in those two months I had come to know several good friends. We get together now and have fun. And suddenly, I realized God had answered a very specific prayer. So not only had you commissioned me, but God had blessed me!"

From Our Home to Yours

Engagement and marriage are among the last events to occur as your child launches into adulthood. The first in our home to be married was our son, Bryan—our middle child. God led him to a great young woman who shares his convictions, faith, and interests and with whom he has a great time.

As we approached the time for the wedding, we wondered what we could do to make the event special and again offer one last *guide-stone moment* that would be memorable as they walked into their new future. We definitely wanted them to go with our blessing and to know that we honored and supported them in this significant step in their lives, but we also wanted to give them a way to be reminded of that reality.

For years, as Bob has officiated at weddings, he has always made sure that the bride and groom understand that the commitment they are making is grounded in the biblical idea of covenant. It's not simply a contract made official by the state in which the ceremony is being held. While covenants are built on trust, contracts are grounded in distrust. Covenants hold high the responsibility of each party, whereas contracts attempt to limit liability.

So Bob points out how aspects of a wedding reflect the concept of a covenant made before God:

- The white runner represents that the site on which the marriage covenant is being made is holy ground.

- The bride and wedding party entering the center aisle with parties sitting on both sides represents the act of passing through the sacrificed animal, as found in Genesis 15, and the seriousness with which the marriage covenant is entered.

- The groom enters first because he is the initiator of the covenant.

- The father walks the bride down the aisle, indicating that the groom is worthy, in his view, of the future for which he raised his daughter. The father is also, in that act, surrendering being his daughter's provider and protector and handing these responsibilities over to the man she is about to wed.

- The groom makes his vows first, representing that from this point on he is to be the spiritual head of the home.

- The couple exchanges rings, indicating that in a marriage covenant everything that is one person's equally becomes that of the other. Life stops being "mine" and "yours"— and it becomes "ours."

- Those present sign the guest book, indicating that they were witnesses of the covenant and will pray for and help hold accountable the two people whose marriage they have helped celebrate and witnessed.

In order to help drive home the reality of this important commitment and to offer a *guidestone marker* to Bryan and his wife, we found a beautiful marriage covenant commitment offered through FamilyLife.

We ordered it on-line from familylifetoday.com and had it lettered in calligraphy and framed, then we awarded it to Bryan and his bride, Ashley (yes, we now have *two* Ashley Reccords in our family!), at their rehearsal dinner. This gave us the opportunity to explain to the guests what covenant relationship is all about, which proved to be a wonderful witness to those present—something we had not even thought about or expected.

You can imagine how thrilled we were when we found this the next day at the wedding reception: displayed on a tripod near the cake was the beautifully framed marriage covenant for all to see and enjoy. Today, it resides in Ashley and Bryan's home as a constant reminder and *guidestone marker* of the covenant they made before God for a lifetime.

Now the Ball Is in Your Court

We have shared these ideas with you, not to add a burdensome amount of work to your already busy and hectic schedule, but to provide samples of things that you can do without radically altering your life to accomplish them. Most of all, we want to stir your creativity in thinking of normal points of passage and transition that happen in the lives of your kids, so you can take opportunities to celebrate rather than let them get by you and later wish you had done something memorable and motivational.

Remember that God told the Israelites as they walked into the Promised Land in Joshua 4 to build a monument of twelve stones to be a constant reminder of how faithful God had been, the many blessings God had given, and the commitment the people had made. Life hasn't changed much: we all still need our markers. May God bless you, parent, as you determine to intentionally and joyfully create your own family markers!

PART II

PRINCIPLES AND PARENTS WHO PRACTICE THEM

CHAPTER 10

EVERYTHING BEGINS WITH A PRESUPPOSITION

PRINCIPLE 1

God prepared a unique plan and calling for your life even before you were born.

Key Scriptures

> Before I formed you in the womb I knew you,
>> before you were born I set you apart;
>> I appointed you as a prophet to the nations. (Jeremiah 1:5)

> For you created my inmost being;
>> you knit me together in my mother's womb.
> I praise you because I am fearfully and wonderfully made.
> (Psalm 139:13–14)

Can you guess what is the most unread book in America? You're probably going to say what you figure is the expected answer: the Bible. But if that's your guess, you're wrong. We came across a survey whose results indicated that the most unread book in America is the car owner's manual! And we can believe that—both of us would go into a coma if we had to read a manual of any kind! In fact, you wouldn't have to convince us that anybody who reads a car owner's manual from cover to cover is in need of counseling.

But when you think about it, the answer makes sense. The car owner's manual is built on a couple of presuppositions. If the owner of the vehicle will read it as a form of preventive maintenance and follow the manual's advice, the car will operate at maximum efficiency and effectiveness and avoid major breakdowns.

Yet when do most of us finally end up reading the car owner's manual? That's right: when our car is broken down on the side of the road. We thumb through it frantically while we wait for the tow truck to arrive.

Regardless of what you're dealing with in life or what belief system you hold, everything is based on presuppositions. It is those presuppositions, by their very nature, that form the foundation and direct the course of everything else in your life. And what better place to find presuppositions—underlying foundational points of absolute truth—than in the Owner's Manual written by the very person who is, Himself, absolute truth?

God's Owner's Manual (the Bible) sets forth a truth very clearly: He had a plan and a calling for every one of us long before we were born. In fact, He says it more than once. And when God says something repeatedly, He's driving home a truth. He wants to make sure we *get it*! He wants us to pass Go and collect two hundred dollars! Just take a minute and read God's Word for your kids (and for yourself, for that matter):

Before I shaped you in the womb,
    I knew all about you.

Before you saw the light of day,
    I had holy plans for you. (Jeremiah 1:5 MSG)

Even then God had designs on me. Why, when I was still in
my mother's womb he chose and called me out of sheer generosity! (Galatians 1:15 MSG)

You made all the delicate, inner parts of my body
    and knit me together in my mother's womb.
Thank you for making me so wonderfully complex!
    Your workmanship is marvelous—and how well I know it.
You watched me as I was being formed in utter seclusion,
    as I was woven together in the dark of the womb.
You saw me before I was born.
    Every day of my life was recorded in your book.
Every moment was laid out
    before a single day had passed.
(Psalm 139:13–16 NLT)

KNITTING YOUR CHILD

Think of it. Right in the womb God was knitting your child together
for a very special purpose and calling. His hands were orchestrating
how your children would look, the talents they would have, the personalities and temperaments they would carry, and the unique
genetic codes they would own. And all that was put together for one
ultimate purpose: so they would come to a point of personally deciding to answer God's call on their lives and fulfill God's plans for their
futures. Now that's an amazing thought.

Consider the marvelous intricacy with which God wove together
your child. While volumes could be filled about the miraculous
aspects of your child's makeup, here are just a few from the weeks
right after conception:

- At fifteen days his heart was forming and his eyes were developing.
- At twenty-four days her heart began to beat.
- At thirty-five days his mouth, ears, and nose were taking shape.
- At forty-three days her brain waves could be recorded.
- At eight weeks the child was well proportioned and every organ was present.
- At twelve weeks the child could kick, curl toes, make a fist, and move his thumbs—he was even breathing!
- At four months she could grasp with her hands and turn somersaults in the womb (much to the mother's chagrin).[1]

And all of that is because God has a plan and a calling to share with each and every child!

When kids lack a sense of destiny—a grounding in purpose for their lives—the results can be devastating. And it gets worse. As the years pass, lack of purpose in life can lead to a lack of desire for life. One study showed this reality with sobering clarity.

Sixty students at an American university were asked why they had attempted suicide. Some 85 percent said life seemed meaningless. However, 93 percent of these students who suffered from apparent lack of purpose were socially active, achieving academically, and on good terms with their families. Yet even in the midst of all of these positive things, they claimed their lives lacked meaning.[2]

MADE TO COUNT

How important it is, therefore, for us as parents to do everything possible to make sure our kids know they were made to count!

But made to count for what? Aha! That's where it gets interesting. In some Christian circles people place a lower value on non-clergy positions of ministry. It's the church's own caste system, and it goes something like this:

- If you're *super*spiritual and *totally* surrendered to God, you'll go to the international mission field.

- If you're *fairly* spiritual and *somewhat* surrendered, you'll become a missionary right at *home* in your own country.

- If you're even a *little* spiritual, yet sensitive to God's calling, then you'll at least surrender to *full-time Christian ministry* or *the pastorate*.

This is tongue in cheek, of course (you knew that, didn't you?). But let's be honest: some folks in the church really have these attitudes, and we must be careful not to let them take root.

We who are parents must be especially careful not to pass along these attitudes to our children. It implies that God isn't ready, able, and willing to use *everyone* who professes His name, and obviously, that's just not true. He can use doctors and mechanics and firemen and teachers and software engineers and home-makers and librarians and pharmacists and artists and—well, you fill in the blank. In fact, people who spend their time in these occupations (and whatever you added to the list) are *essential* to God's kingdom.

And they always have been. Remember the fishermen and tax collectors Jesus called? According to Paul's letter to the Galatians, in Christ "there is neither Jew nor Greek, slave nor free, male nor female, for you are all one in Christ Jesus" (Gal. 3:28). To Paul's list we add one more: in Christ, there is no professional or amateur—we're all equally called to make a difference for Christ's kingdom.

APPRECIATING THE DIFFERENCES

To successfully teach our kids the concept that we're all made to count, we must understand another concept: we're all wired differently. Our Creator gave each of us a different temperament—it's His perfect plan. And it's up to us as parents to recognize and appreciate these different temperaments in our children and to nurture them. We've told you how we found our own kids to be radically different in their makeups: one is a walking social event waiting to happen, the second one is steady and consistent—focused on analyzing detailed issues in life while peppering them with an unbelievably dry wit, and the third is a driven accomplisher, focused on overcoming obstacles. Needless to say, we've never been bored—ready to pull our hair out at times, but never bored!

But it's not enough just to know how our kids are wired; it's important to know how they are different from the way we, as their parents, may be wired. Our friend Mels Carbonell is an outstanding teacher in personality types. He understands how various temperaments can be maximized by interaction with one another. With a doctorate degree, Mels has taught at leading universities around the world. But the most important thing to know about Mels is that he's deeply in love with Jesus Christ. He is the CEO of the Uniquely You Leadership Center and works with us in using the DISC temperament analysis instrument to help adults of all ages better understand how they—as well as their children—are wired and how best to make their temperaments count in relationships.

The DISC instrument divides people into four basic but major temperaments, though it readily acknowledges that each of us is a blend, to varying degrees, of all four.

D—dominant, active/task-oriented, determined, directing, decisive, doing

I—inspiring, active/people-oriented, influencer, impressive, highly interactive and interested in people

S—steady, passive/people-oriented, stable, shy, security-focused, servant, specialist

C—cautious, passive/task-oriented, competent, calculating, detail-oriented, careful, and contemplative

If a person has a lot of scores in one category, we refer to them as a "high D" (or I or S or C). So what happens when a high-D parent gets crosswise with a C-oriented child and tension arises about a decision? Well, we'll let Mels describe such an event in his own journey with his son.

When my oldest son was twelve years old, he asked me if he could do a certain activity. My response was "No." And his natural response was, "Daddy, why can't I do this?"

I don't even remember what the activity was. But it's important for you to keep in mind that I am a high D in my leadership style, and my son is a combination of D, like me, and a high C, like his mother.

So when my only answer was, "Because," I shouldn't have been surprised that it wasn't sufficient. After all, a high C is focused on details, logic, thorough explanations, and arriving at a decision based on understanding the circumstances.

After he thought for a few moments, he realized that my "because" wasn't really an answer. It wasn't logical. It wasn't reasonable. So he responded, "I still don't understand why I can't do it." His challenge was not in a smart-aleck manner—he was simply asking the "whys" of my "because." Now being the nice D that I am (tongue in cheek), I felt as if he was challenging me. So I responded by enlarging my answer: "Because I said so."

And wouldn't you know it, he questioned me again, "But why

just because you say so, Dad?" Again, he wasn't being a smart aleck, but I simply forgot that a high C needs answers that are logical and as thorough as possible. And it was the D in him that was strong enough to come back and question me, but I wasn't taking the time to really listen. Instead, in my high-D directive manner I just commanded, "Go to your room." After all, a child is to do things without murmuring or disputing, to be obedient to the parent and not to challenge him (I was ready to use every Bible verse I could to defend my defective reasoning).

I had tried consistently to be a good dad and give my son focused time and attention. Wasn't that enough? Shouldn't he just be satisfied with my answers? I had even been unwilling to let the Republican National Platform Committee, where I'd been asked to speak several years ago, interfere with my son's soccer game—how's that for a committed dad?

And there he was at age twelve, taking on my amazing reasoning and decision-making prowess. I quickly labeled his actions rebellious, and in my frustration and anger I bit my lower lip. I lost my cool and yelled at him, "Don't challenge me! Don't question me! Just do what I tell you!" As I must have looked foolish in my anger, and biting my lip on top of it, he started to snicker. Rather than seeing how ridiculous I looked and laughing at myself along with him, I simply lost my temper.

I took off my belt and gave him the worst spanking of his life right then and there. He went to his room crying . . . and I went to my room doing the same. I was really upset with myself because I had never lost it like that before. I had spanked him before, but not when I was mad or out of control. I was ashamed.

As I sat in my room alone and reflected back on learning personality temperaments under Dr. John Geyer at the University of Minnesota, I remembered that my son was one of the first personality profiles I did and that he was a D-C. I realized: here I am supposed to be an expert at this personality stuff, and I'm dealing with him as if he's a D like me—and that not very well—when I need to be dealing with the high-C part of him.

I went back to his room and said, "Curtis, I think I did you wrong." His response, not surprisingly, was "You're absolutely right about that, Dad."

And then the two hardest words sometimes for a parent to utter came flowing out of my mouth: "I'm sorry." It's very hard for a high D to say that he is sorry and not use it in a manipulative way. Then I added, "From now on, Curtis, you can laugh at me if I ever bite my lip again. I lost my cool, and I lost my control. I'm very sorry, and I'll never do it again. But I need to explain to you why."

I went on to explain to my son that I had answered his request just to get a decision made, but I understood now that what he needed was a logical reason for my decision. He had to see me, as a parent, admit that I had blown it. Then I added, "You deserve to understand the basis for my decision." I gave him three reasons why I had said no. Amazingly, once I explained, the high-C part of his personality was satisfied.

Some years later when he was home from college, I found myself lying on the floor on a Saturday watching a football game on television. He came in, flopped down on the floor, and laid his head on my chest. I was so excited that he felt comfortable enough to be that close. I thought of Jesus and the apostle John at the Last Supper. I thought of how special what was happening in our relationship was at that moment. Then I started scratching his head, and he simply laughed and said, "Over to the right, Dad. Now over to the left."

With a chuckle I said, "What am I—your pillow?" With that Curtis lifted his head up, leaned on his elbow, looked me straight in the eye, and said, "No, you're my dad!"

I wouldn't take all the money in the world for that moment. But what if I'd never gone back in and understood that he and I are wired differently and made things right when I, as a parent, was wrong?[3]

Go On-Line and Take the Test

Perhaps you'd like a little more information about how you're wired as a parent. In the book Bob wrote with Randy Singer, *Made to Count*—which covers these eight biblical principles applied to the lives of adults—the book owner can go on-line with Mels's organization and complete a free analysis. If you'd like to do that with your own child at this point, turn to just inside the front cover of this book, where you'll find an eight-digit code. Go to the Web site www.uniquelyyou.com, and there you can complete a personality temperament profile for your child. If the child is twelve or older, he or she can do it too with a little help from you. If the child is six to twelve, you've seen enough temperament characteristics up close so that you can take the profile on your child's behalf. Comparing the results for your child with results showing how you're wired will be tremendously helpful to you in learning how best to help your children understand their own "wiring" and grow in decision-making ability.

Let us remind you, this is by no means an infallible instrument! There's only one of those, and that's the Scripture. This is just a simple tool to help you better understand yourself and your children and thus learn how to help them develop into excellent, biblically based decision makers by respecting the way God wired them.

So Principle 1 is *God prepared a unique plan and calling for your life even before you were born.* As parents we need to teach our children to seek that plan and calling and to know that because it's from God, it is good. It is neither inferior nor superior to anyone else's plan and calling. It is good, and it is ours.

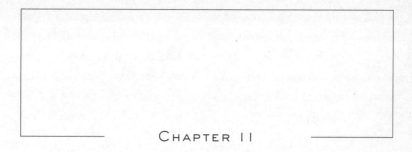

CHAPTER 11

MEET CAROL AND RANDY POPE

God prepared a unique plan and calling for your life even before you were born. No one puts flesh on our first principle better than Randy Pope.

Although many we interviewed prayed for their children before they were born, Randy was doing that even before he married Carol. We like the way he tells it:

> When I was single, I started what I called a Life Notebook. I began to take notes and listen to people who had ideas I admired. I decided I wanted to incorporate those when I became a spouse and a father. I had a whole segment on parenting. So I started trying to work up a game plan, knowing that once the children came I probably wouldn't have time to think.

By working up a "game plan," Randy means developing a vision for how his future children would come to know and serve Christ as their Savior. He made notes to himself on how to develop in his children certain character traits and a hunger for the Lord. He put his notes into categories, such as goals, values, and discipline techniques, that would support his growth as a father. And all this before he was even married!

"As I acquired more ideas and insights from people who inspired me, my notebook grew and developed into a written file on all my beliefs and thoughts and ideas," he says. That makes sense because, to Randy, parenthood is a calling. Randy also developed detailed notations to himself on his calling to be a husband and a minister.

TRILOGIES OF TRUTH

Much of this thinking has found its way into Randy's sermon material at Atlanta's Perimeter Church, where he serves as senior pastor. He is a list maker, and often his lists come in threes—or "trilogies," as he calls them. For example, he's a "strong believer that if you don't have the underpinning of worship, disciple making, and disciple mentoring going on in your experience, then you're not going to be very healthy as a Christian. Those are things I've been passionate about and faithful to pray for for my kids."

Specifically, he asks God to draw them to Him as sincere worshipers, to lead them as faithful disciple makers, and to build them as effective disciple mentors. "I prayed that they would constantly be with lost people trying to tell them about Jesus, and that—once they came to faith and had achieved some spiritual growth—they would always try to find a handful of people to invest their lives in and mentor spiritually."

Another trilogy that he's prayed for consistently for his children: that they would be holy, happy, and healthy. Naturally, his view of health includes spiritual health as well as physical, mental, and emotional. The Popes feel blessed that all four of their children are walking with the Lord, although, because of their individual personalities, some came more quickly to a strong walk than others.

He and Carol developed what they call the Twelve Pope Values. Even when their kids were very young, they homed in on a list that would guide their parenting, especially in a culture that pulls people 180 degrees away from the biblical model. Then they wrote a brief statement to flesh out how each value would manifest itself in their lives. (If you are interested in seeing what some of these values are or getting ideas for crafting your own, go to totallifeimpact.com.)

Keeping the Twelve Pope Values in front of the family was sometimes the basis for a game. One morning Randy came to the breakfast table with a challenge:

> They knew I was tight financially—I never gave them much money. When I did, they always thought it was on the cheap side. But on that day I said, "Guys, I've got a page of Scripture here, and I'm going to make a deal with you. If you memorize this word for word, I will give you . . ." and then I named an amount of money that was so out of character for me that it just about made their eyes pop out of their heads. I told them that the first time they could quote it to me they would get 25 percent of the money. One month later, if they could say it again, they would get the next 25 percent, and so on. So I knew they'd have to keep it in their minds for four months, and by then it would probably never leave them and they'd hold on to the value that Scripture passage was teaching.

The Twelve Pope Values must have made a big impression. That became obvious when Randy and Carol visited their daughter at college and were surprised to find the list framed and hanging over her bed. It's times like that when parents figure out their message really stuck!

We'll close this chapter with more insights from Randy:

- We prayed not only for our children before they were born, but for their spouses. We prayed that each child would find a soul mate with whom he or she could serve Christ.

- We have four kids, all two and one-half years apart from each other; they're now ranging in age from nineteen to twenty-seven. As their schedules became so busy, I had to be deliberate about setting up time to be with each one. I took out each child, maybe for a meal. That time was unstructured in their minds, which was intentional—I didn't want it to appear too engineered to them. I always made the time we were together an opportunity to talk about their lives, their experiences, what they were doing, where they were headed. Then I spent a very short time, typically while we were eating, discussing the Bible. But I always cut it a little short of their expectations rather than let that time go over their expectations. The same was true of our personal worship and devotions as a family. I always wanted to leave them hungering for more, rather than wishing we hadn't gone on so long. Then these studies were just little nuggets, rather than sermons.

- I tried to personalize the nuggets with illustrations from modern life. If we were reading about an adulterous woman, for example, we might discuss how she would look or dress that gave off the message she was a loose woman. We might explore the dangers of flirting and the potential pain of dating a non-Christian person. If we were talking about foolish ways, I shared times I had played the fool in my life, ways I made choices that were not according to God's ways, but man's ways.

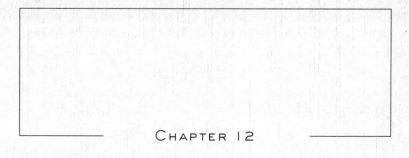

CHAPTER 12

A PERSONAL CALL

PRINCIPLE 2

God calls you to a life-changing relationship with Him through Jesus Christ.

Key Scriptures

> Therefore, if anyone is in Christ, he is a new creation; the old has gone, the new has come! (2 Corinthians 5:17)

> Salvation is found in *no one else,* for there is no other name under heaven given to men by which we must be saved. (Acts 4:12, italics ours)

It was one of those days—a busy Saturday filled with all the activities young families try to cram in: running from Christy's soccer game to Bryan's fall T-ball, then home for Ashley's nap. Cheryl left for the grocery store, and Bob settled in to catch a little college football on TV while getting some work done in his home office and baby-sitting the kids.

That's when it happened. Christy made a mistake—big time! Then, instead of admitting it, she lied. Now, this was the deal in our house: if you lied after breaking the rules, a spanking was always the consequence. Bob realized he was going to have to mete out the discipline. He sent Christy to her room to await her fate, then headed to the family room to give himself some time to cool off. As Bob rounded the corner, there stood Bryan, age six.

"Do you need something, Bry?"

"Christy's in trouble, isn't she, Dad?"

"She sure is!"

Bry went on: "She's dead meat, isn't she?"

"She sure is!"

Then Bryan said something that absolutely floored Bob: "Daddy, would you give me Christy's spanking, so she doesn't have to get it?"

All Bob kept thinking was that if it had been his sister, he'd have been outside her door during the spanking, cheering, "Hit her again, harder! Harder!" And suddenly, God spoke to Bob's heart and whispered: "Do you get it? That's exactly what My Son, Jesus, did for you! When all you deserved was My punishment, Jesus stepped in and said, 'Dad, punish Me instead.'"

Christy received grace that day, and her dad got a life-illuminating illustration of what the gospel is all about—a vivid reminder that we are all sinners, desperately in need of a Savior.

But there is another reality about God's call to a personal relationship with Jesus. It's exactly that—a personal call.

"MOTHER, I'D RATHER DO IT MYSELF"

How many times have we heard our children say that? And in this most critical of all decisions, they are right on target!

Because the decision of what to do with Christ is one that no parent or grandparent, for that matter, can make for a child. Neither can a friend make it. Not even the pastor!

We'll illustrate with some personal background. When Bob was ten, his family attended a church that regularly gave a public invitation at the end of the service for people to make decisions for Christ. One Sunday he sat with his best friend, Gary Vessel. When the response time came, Gary stepped out into the aisle and began to make his way forward. Watching from the pew, Bob saw adult after adult pat Gary on the back as he made his way to the front of the church. Recognizing affirmation when he saw it, Bob set out on his own journey. Sure enough, the adults were congratulatory all along the way.

Reverend Al Smith met both boys with a broad smile. His conversation with Bob went something like this:

"Bobby, are you coming today to make a decision?"

"Yes, sir."

"Bobby, are you coming to accept Jesus Christ into your heart?"

"Yes, sir."

"Do you want to do that right now?"

"Yes, sir."

"Would it be okay if I prayed with you right here on the front pew?"

"Yes, sir."

And pray they did. There was a major problem: the only one who did the praying was the pastor. Of course, his intentions were good. The pastor then filled out a card and announced to the congregation, "Bobby has turned his life over to Christ."

The following week the pastor dropped by Bob's house to talk with his mom and dad, with young Bob as the center of attention. Everybody was thrilled, including Bob. And again the pastor prayed— but Bob didn't.

For the next ten years Bob assumed he was a Christian. He joined the youth choir, was active with the student ministry, became president of the youth group, and even spoke on Youth Sunday before the entire church. He knew Christian lingo. There was only one problem: he still wasn't a Christian. His "decision" and the actions that followed were not personal—they didn't come from his heart.

Scripture is clear that each person must make this decision in his or her own heart, using his or her own mouth: "If *you* confess with *your* mouth, 'Jesus is Lord,' and believe in *your* heart that God raised him from the dead, *you* will be saved. For it is with *your* heart that *you* believe and are justified, and it is with *your* mouth that *you* confess and are saved" (Rom. 10:9–10, italics ours).

The best-intentioned parents or pastors, Sunday school teachers or friends, family members or Christian schoolteachers can, if they're not careful, leave an incorrect assumption. It is vital to lead any child in the opportunity to discover for himself or herself what it means to become a Christian and to have a personal faith in Jesus Christ as Savior—and then to act upon that decision personally. Every parent will want to be sure to put the responsibility where it belongs.

"THERE'S GOT TO BE MORE THAN THIS"

Cheryl grew up in a fine family of active Lutherans, attending church on Sundays and going to a Lutheran school Monday through Friday. Their faithfulness to church was unquestioned. Her focus on learning the basis of their faith never wavered. There was only one problem: all the knowledge in the world did not make a personal relationship with Christ!

When the time came for Cheryl to launch to college, her family was thrilled when, because of her outstanding piano audition, Indiana University invited her to study at its renowned school of music.

But just as important as music and launching into her next phase of skill development, Cheryl had something else in mind. When she got to the campus, she had a prayer conversation with God that went something like this:

> God, there's got to be more to this Christianity than I've seen so far. I know a lot about it, but somehow that doesn't seem very satisfying. I'm going to visit different churches, but I've got to be honest, if I don't find something more, I'm going to forget this religion stuff for good.
>
> By the way, God, I'm not sure You even exist. But if You do, You've got six weeks to prove it to me!

With her task-focused personality, Cheryl didn't see any reason why she shouldn't be as direct with God as she was with life in general!

She kept her promise, visiting a new church every week. By week five, time was running out. Cheryl was ready to admit that the religion thing didn't amount to much after all.

That's when Andy entered her life. A dorm mate, Andy was a vibrant girl with a beautiful smile. One night they had a long talk.

That was the beginning of a brand-new launch and journey for Cheryl. Andy told her about a decision that had changed her life. She talked not about *religion,* but about *relationship.* She explained how religion had to do with things you did or didn't do and the words you said or didn't say. But relationship had to do with intimacy. It involved a growing love affair with the Creator of the universe, who made everyone for a purpose and a plan.

Andy told Cheryl she could know for sure, beyond a shadow of a doubt, that she had a relationship with Him by personally inviting Him into her heart and that, right then, she would be certain of having eternal life when her life on Earth ended.

Thinking she'd heard all the facts about religion, Cheryl was stunned by the idea of a relationship. This one was new to her.

Returning to her room, Cheryl had a lot to think about. But before the night was over and sleep enveloped her into a refreshing rest, she made her decision. She wanted a relationship like that! Privately, in the quietness of her room, Cheryl invited Jesus Christ into her heart as Lord and Savior.

A Joy You Don't Want to Miss

Bob's journey reminds parents that it's important to lead our children so they can make a decision for themselves. It shouldn't be rushed, so that it's not premature. Children should be old enough to understand the decision and follow through with a personal prayer inviting Jesus into their lives—and mature enough to appreciate the significance of what they've done.

Cheryl's journey reminds us that the Bible's instruction on becoming a Christian is based not on *information* but on *relationship*. Children can't go through enough classes to make them Christians. You don't *reason your way* to Christ. It's a decision of the heart, and each person must testify to it by mouth. A parent must understand the difference between facilitating this essential event in the child's life and doing it on behalf of the child.

Through our thirty-plus years of marriage and ministry, we've seen too many parents abdicate one of the most incredible experiences life could ever bring. When a child begins to ask questions about faith, God, what it means to be a Christian, and church, some parents run to the pastor or children's worker to serve as the fount of knowledge for any and every question. As a result, when the child turns his life over to Christ, it happens with someone other than the parent. The child's decision is just as sincere and legitimate, of course, but it robs the parents of one of the greatest experiences they'll have in a lifetime. It's a joy you won't want to miss. It's the *spiritual* birth of your child, and it's a close rival, in satisfaction, to the physical birth.

But . . . But . . . But . . . !

Right about now you may be reading and saying, "But I can't do this. I don't have the theological training to answer the questions, say the right things, avoid mistakes."

We understand your caution and concern. But we have good news for you. God never expected every parent to be a theological expert or New Testament scholar. All He asks is for parents to be loving, to be willing to discuss, and to share from their own personal experiences.

But don't miss this important distinction: parents can *never* share what they don't personally have. So before we go any further, may we ask you: *do you know that you have personally asked Jesus Christ into your life?* Are you convinced, beyond a shadow of a doubt, that He lives in your heart? And do you have complete confidence that you made the decision for yourself?

If you have any question about being sure, we want to help you answer it. If this question lurks in your mind, we invite you to turn to the appendix, "Your Guide to Personal Commitment" and prayerfully determine that you have *personally* made the most important decision in the world—both for yourself and for helping your child do the same.

Okay, Now I'm Sure . . .

Your next question may be "What do I need to know to share Christ with my child?" Here are some guidelines.

- Be open and approachable so you can talk about spiritual things when your child brings questions to the table.

- Don't answer more than the child is asking. We parents sometimes belabor a simple question by telling our children how a watch is made when all they want to know is the time.

- Take it slow. Successfully launching your children—which includes their spiritual rebirth—is not a sprint but a well-run race. Pace the process to be sure your child has a good understanding and comprehension of the basic truths and principles of what it means to have a personal relationship with Christ. Your child does not need an adult's comprehension, just the ability to understand on his or her level and see a need from his or her perspective to make such a decision.

- Acquaint yourself with helpful tools. Maybe you're a parent who doesn't know how to start a discussion with your child about why everyone needs Christ. To help you clearly communicate the gospel to your kids according to their age, we can point you to some great resources made available by the experienced children's evangelism staff of the North American Mission Board. Simply go to our Web site, totallifeimpact.com:

  1. For first- through third-graders and parents to do together, click on "Show and Tell" for an interactive flash presentation.
  2. For preteens, click on the "Cool Stuff for Kids" button. This will bring up an animated on-line video to watch with your child. It's a great discussion starter about what it means to have a personal relationship with Christ. And it can be viewed free of charge.

Or call NAMB at 866-407-6262 to order an inexpensive booklet entitled "An Important Question for an Important Person," which clearly explains the gospel for children in grades 3 through 6.

- The concept of heaven and having the assurance that you'll go there when life on Earth ends may be very real to you as an adult. But remember that from a child's perspective, death and the afterlife are a long time off. Remember this, and also be cautious not to inadvertently give your child a fear of dying. When talking about salvation, emphasize that Jesus, when He comes into your life, gives you a brand-new beginning with a wonderful plan for your future. But He must be *in* your life before you can discover it.

- When dealing with spiritual issues, don't ask questions that your children can answer with a simple *yes* or *no*. Word your questions so that your children will have to give detailed answers; this will assure you that they understand what you're discussing and aren't just giving easy or expected answers.

- Be aware that the church can inadvertently leave the impression at times that the Christian faith is all about "dos and don'ts"—just restrictions. Help your child understand that the Christian faith is the greatest life of freedom possible, if we live within God's safe boundaries. He created these boundaries to protect us and provide us with the best possible life.

We saw this principle fleshed out in our own home. For ten years we had Jack, a beautiful golden retriever. But we lost Jack, much to the grief of our family.

Six months ago our youngest daughter, Ashley, now twenty-one, decided her dad needed a new best friend. Surprising him at home one day, she walked in with an armful of towels. This was not unusual, as she often came by to do some laundry at our house even though she had her own apartment.

When Bob took a closer look at Ashley's laundry, he noticed that it . . . well, it moved! Out squirmed a six-week-old black Labrador retriever puppy. And the love affair began. Her name became Abbey O'Sullivan Reccord, due to Bob's Irish ancestry. We call her Abbey.

Our puppy quickly grew. We got a chain and a screw-in stake for the ground and promptly attached Abbey to it. It was amazing how many things she could get wound around, caught up in, or trapped under.

That's when our neighbors suggested the brilliant idea of an invisible fence. Using a receiver on our porch, we could adjust the electronic signal to allow Abbey a bigger boundary. The battery-equipped collar gave her a mild shock when she wandered too close to the line, warning her of potential danger beyond. After several days of training, she obviously understood and would not go near the boundary. But the amazing thing has been the joyful freedom she's experienced *within* the boundary.

Our neighbors have a golden retriever and suggested we overlap our boundary points. Abbey and Sarah have become best friends, and each can't wait for the other to come out and play. They have total freedom to run in both backyards and to play to their hearts' content within the boundaries of the invisible fence. They're safe and secure but free to enjoy life to the fullest. We've laughed many times at how similar that is to God's provision for us . . . and our children. In His Word He sets boundaries for our protection, safety, and benefit, then He lovingly gives us freedom to move within those boundaries to enjoy life in all its abundance.

That's the kind of picture of God we've tried to convey to our children: being a God of love and grace, He wants to protect us, but in our intimate relationship with Him, He also wants us to experience the wonderful freedom and joy He created for us.

CHAPTER 13

MEET CINDY AND CARLOS FERRER

Life can be full of material riches, but life changes to one of real wealth when we begin a relationship with Jesus Christ. Just ask Carlos Ferrer.

He was born in Havana, Cuba, to a family of successful educators. They worked hard and accumulated wealth along the way. But then Fidel Castro took over the government in 1959, and everything changed. Carlos explains how Castro's regime affected his family:

> The first thing he did when he came to power was to take over the school system, including the private schools, so he could start indoctrinating the children with communism. So that put my family out of business. They confiscated all the land, the building, the buses, the bank accounts—they took everything my family had. We felt we didn't have anything to live for in Cuba.

So as an eight-year-old boy when Castro took over, I went from being in a well-to-do family to not having much. We were in that situation for two years, when finally my father was able to work out a deal to get us to Mexico on a boat. We escaped in the middle of the night. But we had a difficult economic time there too. I had one set of clothes, and the kids starting calling me "Photograph" because I showed up looking the same every day. Hot weather or cold, I wore the same outfit. But that was our new life.

Carlos's family finally came to the United States as refugees in 1962. Life was not great in Miami because so many Cubans were crowded into small spaces. The Ferrers lived in one bedroom that they rented from a family. It had been even worse in Mexico City—there they had shared a two-bedroom apartment with four families.

Faith was not a big factor in their lives. "We went to the Catholic church at Easter and Christmas, but that was about it. There wasn't an emphasis on God in our home." Eventually Carlos's father sought help from the Catholic refugee center. "They wanted to sponsor my family in a move to Minnesota, but my dad said it was too cold there. A friend said that the Baptists were sending families to California. That sounded better to us. So a church in California helped my family with food and jobs and housing. We moved there and started a new life."

Soon his parents learned about having a personal relationship with Christ and were baptized in the church that had sponsored their move. Carlos and his sister did not have this experience, but they received a lot of love and Bibles and clothing for three or four years. Carlos continues:

Later, my family moved to San Antonio, Texas. Finally, I came to know Christ as my Lord when I was a freshman at the University of Texas at Austin. Some friends told me the gospel. They told me I could have eternal life that night and be certain of it. I needed that assurance badly, so I prayed with them to receive Christ. At that moment God showed me why the people at the California church had been so generous to my family: they were thankful for what God had done in their lives, so they were sharing His goodness with us. That became crystal clear to me—it was as if a light bulb of understanding switched on when I prayed that prayer. Later, as I was growing in my faith, I read in the Bible about casting my cares upon Him. That was very comforting to someone who had gone from a life of wealth to rather desperate circumstances. I felt hopeful and secure—rich in a whole new way.

LIFE IN THE BARRIO

Meanwhile, Cindy was growing up in a poor Mexican-American neighborhood, known as a *barrio,* in San Antonio. Unlike her future husband, she had never experienced wealth. In fact, she'd had little exposure to anything or anyone outside the barrio. Says Cindy:

I came to know Christ after seeing a parade—literally! I was sitting in the front yard playing, and a parade of cars came by. I had never seen anything like that. They stopped and told me that Jesus loved me and wanted to have a relationship with me. They invited me to vacation Bible school at their church. I remember the man who was leading that parade. He gave me a big smile and a hug. I wanted to know Jesus, so I showed up at their vacation Bible school and became a Christian that summer.

Ironically, although I knew no one who was wealthy, God had put some really wealthy people in my life to orchestrate that. They paid for me to go to church camp and picked me up in the barrio to attend. Sometimes no one showed up to take me, so I walked. I loved the church classes and needed to be there. My life was full of poverty, but I became rich in spirit. My dad worked four jobs. We lived in a tiny house with my grandparents and my aunt. But

God pulled me through those hard times. And He's been there
ever since.

When Carlos and Cindy married and started their family, they
resolved to make Christ the center. And they saw their parental roles
as being *on mission,* making a conscious effort to share the gospel
with their children. "We wanted to provide a nest, so little birdies
could hatch there and someday be able to fly away with a better
direction in life than we had when we started out," says Carlos, who
now serves as vice president of financial and organizational services
for the North American Mission Board.

No Handbook on Parenting

With no handbook on parenting but caring hearts for children, especially young Hispanics, Carlos and Cindy began reaching out to kids
even before their own were born. Says Cindy: "We worked with barrio kids who didn't have exposure to Christianity. We started witnessing to them. Carlos had a baseball team, and I baked cookies. We
wanted to nurture them, to show them God's love."

The Ferrers depended a lot on prayer and Scripture while rais-
ing their two boys, Al and Drew. It was a learning process, and
Carlos and Cindy grew tremendously in their own spiritual lives.
For example:

Cindy and I spent a lot of time on our knees, but our prayers were
more general until we received such good counsel from our friend
Sarah. "Are you praying *specifically* for Al's dyslexia?" she asked.
That blew me away! So we began praying that Al would not
become discouraged, that he would realize that God never makes
junk, that we and his teachers would be able to build on the fact
of his incredibly high IQ to give him confidence, even though
learning was difficult at times.

Today both boys are married men with Christian wives and families, living within five miles of their parents. Both serve Christ in their work, one as a software salesman in a dog-eat-dog world where he's often the only one operating with a sense of fairness and ethics, and the other as a coach and teacher at a high school. There he sees kids every day with huge problems. But he felt called to leave a successful career in the computer business to follow Christ into a new career ministering on His behalf.

We'll close with other insights from the Ferrers:

Carlos: We shared our home with a lot of kids. I think in our community our home was known as the place where kids were welcome, whether they were happy or sad, whether good things were happening in their lives or they were going through troubles. After Friday night football games, there was always a party at our house. It was nonalcoholic, but we had plenty of pizzas. We also had prayer. If it was Saturday, they'd spend the night. Then they'd go to church with us the next morning. The condition was: "We feed you, you sleep here, in the morning we all go to church together."

Cindy: One thing that stretched us spiritually as a family was hospital visits, especially to AIDS patients. This was in the early days of AIDS, and people were scared of catching it, even healthcare workers. But I remembered the verse in Matthew 25:40: "I tell you the truth, whatever you did for one of the least of these brothers of mine, you did for me." And I felt it was important for us to care for these people and to pray that God would honor that by keeping us healthy. Sometimes I wouldn't mention to Carlos and the boys until after our visit that the patient had AIDS. I wanted them to see the person— his heart and soul, as God sees him.

Carlos: I remember asking Cindy, "Why are we paying twenty dollars for one red plate?" But she had a great idea for how to use it, and it's paid for itself many times over in happy, motivational moments. Whenever a child had something special to celebrate—good grades, or he had memorized a Scripture—he found the red plate at his place at the table.

Cindy: Carlos had what he called the Show Me program. When the boys did something wrong, to get them back on course or to earn back the right to do certain things, he told them, "You blew it. Now you're going to have to Show Me you're responsible." What made it work so well was Carlos's consistency and the fact that he did it with love.

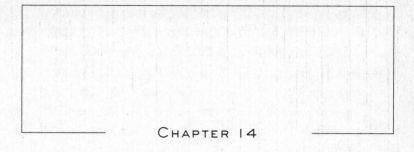

CHAPTER 14

THE ULTIMATE MISSION

PRINCIPLE 3

God calls you to partner with Him in a mission that is bigger than you are.

Key Scriptures

> Now glory be to God! By his mighty power at work within us, he is able to accomplish infinitely more than we would ever dare to ask or hope. (Ephesians 3:20 NLT)

> I can do everything through him who gives me strength. (Philippians 4:13)

> David said to the Philistine [Goliath], "You come against me with sword and spear and javelin, but I come against you

in the name of the LORD Almighty, the God of the armies
of Israel, whom you have defied. This day the LORD will
hand you over to me, and I'll strike you down and cut off
your head. Today I will give the carcasses of the Philistine
army to the birds of the air and the beasts of the earth, and
the whole world will know that there is a God in Israel. All
those gathered here will know that it is not by sword or
spear that the LORD saves; for the battle is the LORD's, and
he will give all of you into our hands." (1 Samuel 17:45–47)

A mission bigger than you are. Sounds overwhelming and daunt-
ing, doesn't it? What comes to your mind when you think of those
words? Is it finding a cure to a deadly disease . . . leading a team in a
victorious venture . . . standing steadfast against overwhelming odds
. . . or launching into the unknown, like the brave astronauts who
are thrust into the depths of space?

Those grandiose ideas are natural. But in our opinion, they don't
begin to touch one of the greatest missions of a lifetime: raising children who know they are made to count and have a mind-set to give
themselves away in the service of their Creator and fellow man. An
investment in that significant, life-changing mission can make all the
difference in the world—for us as parents, for our kids, and for every
life they may touch.

And if you don't believe us, just look at two families from history.
One set of parents embraced the most significant mission of their lives
by raising kids with an *on mission* mind-set to change their world. The
other set wasted their opportunity, and the results speak for themselves.

THE EDWARDSES AND THE JUKES

Jonathan and Sarah Edwards lived in the early 1700s. He is best
known as a Puritan leader who had an amazing impact in the revival

movement known as the Great Awakening. His sermon "Sinners in the Hands of an Angry God" is one of the best known in history.

While Jonathan was focused, serious, and studious, Sarah was vibrant, kind, and a gracious extrovert. They had eleven children (that's right, eleven!). Mornings began early in the Edwards household with prayer and a chapter of Bible reading by the father, who asked God's blessing and guidance for the day. Each child had responsibilities to perform. No one got a free ride, because Mom and Dad understood that responsibility contributes to maturity. And they taught each child to relate to others with courtesy, respect, and graciousness.

Jonathan Edwards took fathering seriously. He gave at least one hour each day to focusing his attention on the children. During that time they could ask any question they wanted, get help with any problems, or pursue any other interests with their dad. Quite a contrast when studies tell us that today's father spends less than three minutes a day of focused attention on his children.

The Edwards children saw their parents expressing love and affection to one another. On afternoons of good weather, Jonathan and Sarah rode together on horseback to spend quality time strengthening their relationship and allowing their children to see this priority. While they were surely not wealthy in worldly goods, they were absolute millionaires in family relations, spiritual depth, and love for others.

In 1900, A. E. Winship researched hundreds of Edwards descendants and reported these results:

- Thirteen college presidents
- Sixty-five professors
- One hundred lawyers and a law-school dean
- Thirty judges
- Sixty-six physicians and a medical-school dean

- Eighty holders of public office, including three U.S. senators, three mayors of large cities, three state governors, a U.S. vice president, and a comptroller of the U.S. Treasury
- 135 books written by descendants
- One hundred missionaries and members of mission boards[1]

On the other end of the spectrum were the descendants of a Dutch immigrant who lived in the early 1800s. Sociologists refer to him as Max Juke. A study was conducted in 1877 of this family who populated a county in New York. These parents were beset by many problems. But judging from how their descendants turned out, it appears they failed to grasp that the most exciting mission of their lives was to build children with deep spiritual, emotional, and intellectual roots who would then gain wings to change their world. Instead, they let the kids rule the roost; they chose not to "warp their psyches" with discipline and not to impose restrictive boundaries of any kind. As a result, the family's legacy is quite different.

- Three hundred professional paupers
- 130 convicted criminals
- Ninety prostitutes
- Twenty learned a trade, but ten of them were trained in prison[2]

So as you're reading, just take a moment and think: the greatest mission you have is the mission of building great kids.

PAYING THE PRICE TO TURN THE TIDE

Bob doesn't have to read stories of the Jukes' descendants to know that family choices, good or bad, have a huge effect on everyone who follows. Bob's name before adoption was Sullivan. It stretches all the way back to the O'Sullivan clan from Ireland. As we've gotten to know historical facts of his lineage, we are amazed and gratified to learn what God has done to bring him where he is.

- Each generation had several alcoholics.

- Bob's biological father was an alcoholic.

- Bob's adoptive father was an illegitimate child as a result of an indiscretion by a married man with a young woman.

- The mother of Bob's adoptive dad was caught being unfaithful and shot by her own husband.

- Bob's uncle was killed by an angry husband with whose wife he'd had an affair.

But Bob's adoptive mother, Ruth, was determined to turn the tide. Though she broke her mom and dad's heart when she married a non-Christian, she was determined to make the marriage work. And with the help of her pastor, she saw her rough-edged husband make a commitment of his life to Christ. He worked hard at striving to be a decent, hardworking man, committed to providing Bob with an environment in which he could find God's perfect plan for his life.

Perhaps your background has been less than ideal. Maybe you weren't raised in a *Leave It to Beaver* family, and you didn't have a *Father Knows Best* home. And just maybe some of the breaks in your life haven't gone the way you wish they had. But the turn for your family's future can begin with *you*. It won't be easy, but it begins with your commitment to turn the tide with God's guidance.

LOUD ACTIONS

One thing we parents learn quickly is that our actions speak louder than our words. We can try to teach patience, but if we fly off the handle with our kids, our lesson is lost. We can talk about sharing and its importance and yet refuse to share our time with our kids due to busy schedules, demands, job responsibilities, and phone calls.

When we first came across the incredible histories of the Edwards family and the Jukes, they jumped off the page to us: one set of parents modeled to their children a life focus that was eternal, while the other set zeroed in completely on the temporal. The Edwards couple believed that transformed lives and a better society were a legacy worth leaving while, apparently, the Jukes weren't even worried about legacy.

This made us realize that Christ-following parents need to talk in front of their kids—at dinner, in the car, when they're just hanging out together—about how they believe the eternal things of life are by far the most important investment one makes. Ironically, we've discovered that many parents find it easier to talk about their personal sense of mission with friends, fellow church members, and even work associates than with their own children. Yet no one needs to hear it more from Mom or Dad than the children who live with them.

Also, it's amazing what reading does in the life of a child, especially if the parents start when the kids are young. It brings into their lives a sense of adventure, imagination, belief, and even faith. The Bible itself proclaims, "Faith comes by hearing, and hearing by the word of God" (Rom. 10:17 NKJV).

What greater investment could parents or family members make than to read to their children the great stories of mission from the Bible? It's as though God crafted many of those stories with kids in mind, building within their hearts a sense of being *on mission* from an early age. Stories about the young brother Joseph in Genesis, Daniel being taken into captivity as a young man, and the teenager David running up against the giant in his life, Goliath: all grab the imagination and faith of young people to believe that God can help them do what otherwise would be impossible, and that without Him many of the challenges of life are just that—impossible.

Bob still remembers clearly how his mother, as well as an aunt, read to him these great stories and others from the Bible as he was growing up. Imbedded in his memory bank is a family Bible with black-and-white pictures of many great scenes in the stories. That Bible's stories began to build into Bob's life from an early age the belief that God had an exciting plan for his life, just as He did for many people in Scripture. With today's picture Bibles and illustrated Bible software, it's never been easier to convey the great stories of faith and mission to our kids.

As your kids grow older, challenge them to read biographies and autobiographies of great leaders in the Christian world. We recommend *Daws,* the story of Dawson Trotman, who founded the Navigators, by Betty Lee Skinner; *Amazing Faith* by Michael Richardson (the authorized biography of Bill Bright); *The Billy Graham Story* by John Pollock; *America's Christian Heritage* by Gary DeMar (the stories of some of America's founders and their faith). In addition to books on the lives of missionaries and other great church leaders, bookstores offer biographies of Christians in sports, business, and the arts. Reading these will provide great balance and perspective for a teen moving quickly toward adulthood.

If you challenge your teens to read these biographies, don't forget to find time to discuss what they're discovering through their reading. Your teens will relate better to these people if you give them a chance to articulate the lessons they're seeing in the lives of these Christians.

EXPERIENCES OVER THINGS

A friend who's a bit older than we are told us years ago, "Don't be as concerned about giving your kids things as you are about sharing with them experiences. Things will be discarded, but the experiences will live in their hearts forever." What great advice! We find that many kids who seem to be developing a healthy *on mission* perspective on life have family members who either accompany them on mission trips or otherwise make sure they have a rich variety of mission experiences. Bob annually spends a week speaking at Student Leadership University in Washington, D.C., and in London. These are some of the sharpest, most committed young adults you will ever meet! These kids say mission experiences—especially those shared with family members—are what radically impact their lives, demonstrating to them the principle that *God calls you to partner with Him in a mission that is bigger than you are.* It's learning by doing.

One of our greatest memories is taking Ashley on a World Changers trip, where students and parents give a week of their lives to rebuild housing in urban areas and, in the process, have the opportunity to share Christ with residents. The program in 2004 included nearly twenty-five thousand high-school participants. To this day Ashley tells us, "Until that time in my life, I'd always heard about being *on mission* and been told the importance of being *on mission,* but that's the first time I ever understood what it felt like to be *on mission.*"

Have you heard of Prison Fellowship's Angel Tree Christmas program? We know many parents and grandparents who do a great job of getting their kids involved in Angel Tree. They buy Christmas presents and donate some of their own for children of prisoners. Others take their kids on mission trips in North America and overseas. Still others focus on local opportunities such as soup kitchens, where kids learn to give themselves away to those far less fortunate than they are. It's healthy for kids to realize from firsthand experience how blessed they are, even *with* a mom and dad who don't let them do every single thing they want to do—in fact, they discover that's part of the blessing.

Out of parents' examples will come children's desires to be involved in *on mission* experiences on their own or with their classmates. Randy and Rhonda Singer, dear friends of ours, have modeled an *on mission* lifestyle to their two kids since Rosalyn and Josh were youngsters. Now they're in their late teens and early twenties and are giving themselves away both in North America and overseas in places such as Beirut, Lebanon, and Aguadilla, Puerto Rico. And both are convinced that God has special plans for their lives. They learned this *on mission* attitude by example from parents who know that *God calls them to partner with Him in a mission that is bigger than they are.*

ROLE MODELS

Remember, Mom or Dad, this kind of mind-set is *caught* much more than it is *taught*. Take every opportunity to get your kids around the kinds of adults you want them to become. Look for opportunities to have adults visit in your home who have the worldview and life perspective you want your kids to develop. We were fortunate early in our journey as parents to have adults who took an interest in our kids. We try to return the favor whenever possible.

Bob was asked to lead chapel for the Tampa Bay Buccaneers. Doug Gilcrease, Bucs chaplain, invited Bob to stay at his home rather than at a hotel. Doug told Bob: "I love to have my kids around adults who believe in Christ and His purpose for their lives just as their Mom and Dad do. Sometimes they'll hear it even more strongly from people *other* than Mom and Dad. I find that the reinforcement of hearing what we already say to them is amazing."

With that kind of invitation, Bob couldn't resist and had a ball staying there and focusing on the kids. And it's true: if you want your kids to really *hear* what you're saying, help them hear it from other adults whom they respect or have fun with.

Well, it sounds easy, doesn't it? But then so does dieting! The bottom line for all of us as parents is not merely knowing what to do, but *just doing it.*

And here's what happens when our kids develop an *on mission* mind-set, perspective, and lifestyle: they learn that it's not all about them—it's all about Him!

CHAPTER 15

MEET MARY AND
RON JENSON

How do you teach little ones a concept as big as *God has a mission for your life that's bigger than you are?* Children are, by definition, small. And part of their nature is to be self-centered, at least until they begin to learn about the world around them.

Meet the Jensons. They made it a point to teach their two kids that "you can be all Christ wants you to be wherever you are, doing whatever you're doing," as Ron puts it.

We've been careful to instill the concept that all of life is ministry. It doesn't matter where you get your paycheck, and it doesn't matter what you do for a living. You live and walk in the power of the Spirit. You share Christ by word and by deed and by love. And you certainly don't have to be in full-time ministry to be used by Him in a full-time way. I think teaching this is one of the larger gifts we've been able to give our kids.

One way the Jensons taught it was by exposing their kids to lots of people and experiences: leaders, thinkers, people who challenged them to grow. The Jensons believe kids become like the people with whom they spend quality time. Explains Ron:

> There's a school of thought that says there's behavioral transformation that happens through cognitive change, and then there's sociological transformation that happens in the context of the body. So we have forever exposed them to friends. We've tried to make our home the kind of place where our kids' friends would feel welcome, so we could influence them a bit as well.

A missionary family lived with them for more than a year, which allowed the Jenson kids to see up close and personal some folks with hearts for Cambodia, who could live on pennies and didn't care about money. But even with this family in the home, Mary and Ron emphasized that missions work doesn't require overseas travel, realizing, as Mary says, "There's lots of work in the kingdom."

THE BUSINESS-PLAN WEEKEND

Effectively communicating this kind of attitude takes some deliberate planning. Mary encourages moms she mentors to get away with their husbands and have what she calls a Business-Plan Weekend for their kids. "We do it in the corporate world all the time: you make an assessment of your business and do the profit-and-loss analysis. Too many well-meaning couples just don't think about doing that for their families—having a retreat to address the needs of their kids."

She and Ron used to take off for a weekend and talk about areas where they felt they needed to give their kids more guidance—anything from manners to discipline to spiritual issues. They tried to take a trip away at least twice a year for that purpose.

It gave us a framework so we could think strategically about how
we were going to parent them. Remembering that we have two
kids, a boy and a girl with vastly different personalities, we wrestled
with the reality that how we parented or disciplined one just didn't
work for the other. So we really needed to take time away to think
about it.

Adds Ron:

Businesses never really move ahead without a good business plan.
Successful ministries have a good strategic plan. But people sel-
dom develop one for their families, and it's a shame. We decided
early on that we would be different, more intentional, because we
had certain outcomes we wanted for our children: a sense of mission in their lives based on a passion for Christ and the kingdom
in the broadest sense of the term, whether they wound up in business or politics or education or professional ministry. We taught
them that it really doesn't matter where you get paid. All occupations and pursuits can be ministry.

The Seven Fs

The Jenson couple came up with a list of values, all beginning with
the letter *F:* faith, fitness, family, friends, finances, future, and fun.
They went so far as to have their children write out things to accomplish in those categories, "to make sure they were aiming in that
direction. Our observation has been that if people don't start thinking about these as kids, they may never get around to it as adults,"
says Ron.

We'd go through an exercise. We'd say, "Imagine you're eighty years
old, and you're sitting in a rocking chair looking back on your life.
What would it look like in the area of faith? How have you lived

your life for the Lord? How well do you know the Bible? How has God's Word affected your life? What about friends and family? Have you helped them experience the fullness of the Spirit?"

The bottom line of all this was to give them the mind-set that life is really a race—not a sprint, but a marathon. Paul said in 1 Corinthians 9:24, "In a race all the runners run, but only one gets the prize. Run in such a way as to get the prize." Then in 2 Timothy 4:7–8 Paul said, "I have fought the good fight, I have finished the race, I have kept the faith. Now there is in store for me the crown of righteousness." Again, we wanted our son and daughter to get into their spirits pretty deeply the reality of those concepts.

We'll close with more of their wisdom:

Ron: When Matt was eight, he and I began going to Bob's Big Boy. We took *The Living Bible* with us, and we read eight to ten verses. We color-coded the verses: yellow for the tongue, green for the things you should do, blue for things you shouldn't do, and red for the heart and the mind. That really bonded us as father-son, and it also gave him a perspective on skills for living. Eventually, we wrote a book together on fathers and sons. I think the heart of it started with those meals and Bible lessons at Bob's Big Boy.

Ron: Some boys mature early in sports and physical abilities, while others mature later. But peer pressure can be overwhelming, especially if the boy's gifts are in the areas of artistic abilities, intellectual pursuits, and the development of ideas over brawn. It's critically important to continually build up a boy like that by showing him the importance of his particular strengths, assuring him that he will also develop physically and come into his own as a man. One thing we know is that you don't try to create your child in your own image. You try to help him find who God made him to be.

Well, Matt started to play the piano. I played catch or shot hoops with him, just to round him out, but I was careful not to try to make him into the athlete I was or wanted to be or, at some level, even achieved. I think that's a horrible mistake too many dads make. Finally, I took him to a Promise Keepers event, where I was a speaker. He was just going into high school, and he became convicted at PK that he needed to start a small group for prayer.

I asked him: "Who will you go after for your group?" He said he wasn't sure. I suggested he seek out some of the leaders on campus. So he did. He even invited the student body president. He brought them to our home, and they prayed on Sundays.

He started out with three, then six, then eight, then into the larger numbers. Most of them were unbelievers. One day I asked Matt, "How do you get these guys here to pray for a couple of hours?" He told me his technique. "I ask them what their relationship is like with their dad. They all tell me the same thing—pretty much terrible. So I suggest we pray about that." The bottom line is that he started ministering to these kids, and he grew and developed and gained confidence. When you're good at one thing, you start feeling better about yourself. That happened to Matt. By the time he was a senior, he had had an impact on so many kids' lives.

Ron: Christian parents struggle with how to counter a culture that's moving 180 degrees in the opposite direction. One of my vivid memories is when Matt was in high school. He had grown up not being very socially astute, but when he got to high school, he became more and more popular because he was ministering to so many kids. So at homecoming there were thousands of people in the stands. The homecoming court was announced, and Matt was named a prince. Mary and I knew that ahead of time so we would be ready at half-time to walk the fifty-yard line with him and the other court members.

When we walked out to join him, Mary was on one side and took his hand or looped her arm through his—I forget which. He reached out for my hand, but I thought, *He doesn't really want to do this . . . too many people here . . . I don't want to embarrass him.* So I just hit his elbow with my elbow, then stuck my hand in my pocket. He was the only nonjock or non-student-body officer on the court, yet he was named the homecoming king.

It was a great night, one of the highlights of his youth. The next day Mary came to me and said, "Honey, do you know how much you hurt your son last night?" I asked what she meant. Women have an antenna. They are aware of all the things going on around them. Guys have little peepholes we look through. Or maybe it's like binoculars—we're just look-ing straight ahead, and we're not aware of things around us the way women are.

Mary said, "When he reached out to hold your hand, he actually wanted to do it! He wanted to demon-strate to all his friends, plus the parents and teachers and administrators who knew him, how much he and his dad love each other. They knew it, of course, but he wanted to show it nonverbally."

I was flabbergasted. I had let the culture lead me 180 degrees away from what it means to be a real man. I was filled with the macho view of being a father and being a man, and I didn't follow my son's lead that night and let him express his message or have the impact he wanted to make.

I went to Matt and apologized. He was very gracious in his response, but that experience totally changed me. Ever since that day I realized that I could never again be conformed to the world. A real man is both tough and tender. He's affectionate; he's loving. It was a great lesson, and I was the learner.

Mary: We found that there came a point when our children's dependence on us was not enough; they needed to learn to trust God. It happened in our daughter's life when she was about twelve, and we began to do a bit of traveling—two or three trips a year for maybe three to five days at a time. It wasn't a lot, but it was a time in Molly's life when she'd begun to realize how fragile life is. It became difficult for her when we traveled. She actually had panic attacks. I realized I was going to have to find a whole new way of relating to her.

So knowing one particular trip was coming up, I took an empty book and put into it Scriptures that were most comforting to me when I was fearful. I typed them on my computer, printed them out, and pasted them into this book. I left blank pages between each one, so she could journal her thoughts and feelings and prayers while we were gone. This was when 1 Corinthians 10:13 became her life verse: "No temptation has seized you except what is common to man. And God is faithful; he will not let you be tempted beyond what you can bear. But when you are tempted, he will also provide a way out so that you can stand up under it."

I think the principle here is that when you see your children struggling, you can show them how to apply the Word to that struggle and then help them make the extrapolation into other parts of their lives. Molly has seen me do it when I've felt fearful about travel too. In fact, one time when she was only a high-school freshman, she was flying solo from San Diego to Minneapolis in the winter with bad weather all around. I woke up about 3 AM freaking out, thinking of every imaginable bad thing that could happen. So I got up and prayed through Psalm 91, a psalm about protection, but somehow even that made me nervous. Finally, my eyes drifted across the page in my Bible to Psalm 95:8–11 where God says, in essence, "Stop testing Me! I've taken care of this child for fourteen years. Why do you think I'm going to stop now?"

The next day I showed Molly what the Lord had shown me through that verse. She looked up at me with her little tear-stained face, and by the time she got out of the shower that morning, she was singing. It was a period in her life when there didn't seem to be much I could do for her, but I could direct her to the Word and what the Lord could do for her.

Ron: We had a course correction with Matt, when he was just beginning to move into the teen years. We did what we often did in the summers: vacationed with friends, in this case, Barbara and Dennis Rainey of FamilyLife. Well, Dennis and I decided to take our two sons on a fishing trip. But really, the purpose was The Big Sex Talk. Dennis and I, being the pros that we are in the area of marriage and family life [smile], decided to play the James Dobson *Preparing for Adolescence* tapes.

We were driving along on the freeway with the men in the front and the boys in the back, listening to Dobson's tape where he deals with sexual issues head on: physical relationships and thought patterns, puberty and masturbation, sensitive issues like that. Our boys were—we found out later—rolling their eyes and going, "What in the world have our dads gotten us into?" Dennis and I played a tape, and then we tried to talk about it a little bit. We asked questions, and there was utter silence in the backseat.

We finally got through the tapes, and we did have some discussions about what it means to be a young man and to be pure. But one question they asked us really stood out. They wanted to know if we had been true to our wives, which was a really astute question for kids their age. We told them that we absolutely had. That discussion probably had a greater impact on them than anything else we said.

Ron: We had a course correction with our daughter. After she'd been in college for about a year and a half, Molly decided that she didn't want to finish. That surprised us, because we'd made a big deal out of her going to school. We had both gone through college, doing graduate and postgraduate work. And Matt had graduated and was going on with his PhD. It never occurred to us that Molly wouldn't want to finish college, but the fact of the matter was she had the opportunity to travel around the country and sing with a Christian rock band.

We said: "Molly, we love you, and we're supportive of whatever you want to do. But even if you go into ministry, college will help. In fact, if you want to go into Campus Crusade, you'll have to be a college graduate." We addressed all the pros and cons we could think of.

At the end of the day, she decided she still wanted to take off with a band and spend a year on the road. So the course correction was for her to drop out of school. We reasoned with her and did as much as we could, then we left it up to the Lord. As you know, we both think it's important that you don't try to create your kids in your own image.

Well, the net effect of all that is that Molly did go on to do about three hundred concerts that year for junior high and high school kids. She traveled in a van with a group of people and lived in other people's homes. She made very little money, but she ministered her heart out. She honed her musical, performance, and ministry skills, and she led kids to Christ in the process. It was a much more intensive education than she could have gotten in college.

She had a sense of what God was calling her to do. It was something bigger than her and even bigger than college, and she followed Him. Many have come into the kingdom, and I'm sure many more will in the days to come. She's having a multiplication impact. That's big.

CHAPTER 16

WHAT ARE YOU
WAITING FOR?

PRINCIPLE 4

God calls you to be *on mission* with Him right where you are—starting now.

Key Scriptures

> Those tending the pigs ran off and reported this in the town and countryside, and the people went out to see what had happened. When they came to Jesus, they saw the man who had been possessed by the legion of demons, sitting there, dressed and in his right mind; and they were afraid. Those who had seen it told the people what had happened to the demon-possessed man—and told about the pigs as well. Then the people began to plead with Jesus to leave their region.

As Jesus was getting into the boat, the man who had been demon-possessed begged to go with him. Jesus did not let him, but said, *"Go home to your family and tell them how much the Lord has done for you, and how he has had mercy on you."* (Mark 5:14–19, italics ours)

As Jesus walked beside the Sea of Galilee, he saw Simon and his brother Andrew casting a net into the lake, for they were fishermen. "Come, follow me," Jesus said, "and I will make you fishers of men." (Mark 1:16–17)

But you will receive power when the Holy Spirit comes on you; and you will be my witnesses in Jerusalem [right where you are], and in all Judea and Samaria, and to the ends of the earth. (Acts 1:8)

The buzz in the Starbucks was hypnotic. It reflected today's town square, with most people communicating electronically. Some tapped furiously on laptops; others punched messages onto the tiny keyboards of hand-held BlackBerries. The aroma of freshly brewed coffee filled the air.

Three women huddled in a corner—good friends—sharing deeply from their hearts.

Brittany, with her dark hair clipped back, wore loose-fitting cargo pants, a tee shirt, and sneakers. She took a big gulp of java and turned to her compatriots. "It's just not the way I thought it would be. Ever since I became a Christian, I've envisioned myself standing in front of an audience of women as I deliver a life-changing message. In my mind I could just see them sitting on the edges of their chairs, hanging on every word, pens flying across pages of notes . . . and, of course, the tons of applause! You know, like Beth Moore! And now as a mom at home with three kids, the only thing I have tons of is dirty clothes. You two have it so much better. Your lives are together! And you're both making such a difference."

Paige, in her silk pantsuit, looked as if she'd stepped off the cover of a business magazine. She shook her head in disbelief. "Brittany, what are you talking about? You've got three of the greatest kids I've ever seen. When I see you laughing with them as you dash off to a soccer game or a ballet recital, I have to admit, I'm jealous."

Paige's eyes grew moist. "Jim and I have been trying for so long to have a baby . . ." She paused, fumbling with her cup. "We just learned we've got a fertility problem—and it looks as if we'll never have our own children. It's a real shock to us." Paige fell quiet, gathering strength. "I like my work, but compared to raising children, the marketplace isn't all it's cracked up to be. Besides, even with my track record in sales, I still don't feel as if I've come close to what you've done, Suzanne." Paige glanced at the third coffee-klatch partner. Suzanne was already a domestic court judge at the age of thirty-six.

"Thanks for the compliment, Paige. It means so much." Suzanne placed her hand gently over Paige's and gave her friend a tender smile. Then she sighed and withdrew her hand. "Remember, everything that glitters isn't gold. On the outside, I may look like a success. But before you go there, let me tell you the rest of the story."

Suzanne paused, as if considering whether vulnerability was such a good idea. "I've worked hard to get where I am. Sure, I sit as judge on a domestic court bench, but I'd give anything to have Brad back as my husband. I didn't realize the price you pay when you get caught up in a demanding job. You can lose track of your priorities. I didn't really stop loving him, but my focus on career got in the way . . ." Her voice cracked. "Then I realized he'd stopped loving me."

Brittany jumped in to lighten the mood and encourage her friend. "But, Suzanne, you just seem to be so together. I've never seen anything too hard for you, and you take everything in stride. I don't know how you do it. You'll have men lining up to take a number in no time."

Suzanne nodded her appreciation, then glanced away. She

gathered control of her emotions, calling on her specialty—self-discipline. Life hadn't turned out quite as she'd imagined as a starry-eyed law student. She'd dreamed of a small private practice with manageable hours and a family life filled with laughter, shared experiences, and deep affection.

"I may look as if I have it all together and everything comes easy, but the truth is I'm barely surviving. I hop out of bed at 5:30, dress, and make my daughter's lunch for school. Then I gobble down oatmeal and dry toast as I do last-minute cramming for the docket I'll face that day.

"When Jennifer bounds down the stairs, she wants my full attention. That's what happens at age ten, and she talks nonstop as we race to the bus. That girl can run and talk without breathing!

"That's when I run to my car and beat it to the court, where I slip into my chambers, don a robe, and head to the bench. And from that moment on, I hear case after case after case. Cases that break my heart. Hour after hour I'm deciding whether to take a child from his or her parents, whether to declare aging seniors incompetent, whether a mentally ill spouse should be committed, whether to grant a divorce. It just seems to go on and on and on.

"On good days I get out of chambers by 6:30. That's when I race home, usually making a quick stop at the grocery store. When I arrive about seven, I help my mom finish dinner, get it on the table, eat with her and Jennifer, and then I clean everything up.

"After dinner we dive into Jennifer's homework and slave over that till bedtime strikes. Then it's tuck her in and have our prayers.

"When I collapse on the couch, my mom's ready to talk. She's great being there to help take care of Jennifer, but there are times I wish I could sit in silence. I'm surrounded by so much sound all day long.

"Finally, it's off to a quick bath—no bubbles for me—then fall into bed and read briefs for the next day's cases. After a few hours of sleep, it starts all over again."

Suzanne slumped as if just reciting her schedule had worn her out. "I feel as if I need a mixed drink of Ensure and Geritol just to keep going. And deep in my heart, I really want to make a difference for God, but I don't see how! Where would I find time?"

Brittany nodded, a half-smile playing on her lips. "You know, I'm just so thankful to be able to sit here and talk to you both as adults. I love my kids with all my heart, but sometimes, as I stay at home with them day after day, I feel as if my brain is turning to mush. As a college graduate, I never thought my days would be filled with Big Bird on *Sesame Street* teaching me how to dance."

The sound of a muffled Dixie tune caught Brittany's attention, and she reached for her cell phone. Digging to the bottom of her purse, which was no small task, she finally pulled it out. Her husband, Chad, had left her a message, and his voice sounded deep and resonant: "Hi, babe. I just want you to know I love you and appreciate all that you do. I'm glad you're out with the girls having a great time. I'll look forward to seeing you when we both get home later tonight. Know that I love you."

As she jammed her phone back into the Bermuda Triangle of her purse, Brittany looked first at Paige and then at Suzanne. Her eyes danced with anticipation. "Listen, ladies, all of us have our challenges. And I love a good pity party as much as anybody, but let's get a grip. What we need is a new perspective. Suzanne, you're a single working mom. Paige, you're a working wife. And I'm a stay-at-home mom. But one thing I know is that all of us can make a difference for Christ." Her friends were giving her that what's-got-into-you look, but Brittany felt an energy seeping into her voice. Okay, maybe it was the caffeine, but still . . .

"We need to start looking at how to do it in ways that don't just tack on new activities in our lives but make use of opportunities we already have. What if we evaluated our lives—could some things be tweaked or changed? But, hey, if that's too hard, then let's assume most of it will stay the same. Where can we find areas that can piggyback with an opportunity to be *on mission* for Christ?

"For example, Christmas is coming. Suzanne, since you and I live in the same community, why don't we get together and throw a birthday party for Jesus? We'll invite kids on our street. Just explaining what will happen at the party will start conversations with the parents. Paige, you live in a neighborhood filled with upwardly mobile women. There's got to be a creative way for you to reach out and touch those around you."

She had the attention of her friends, but the skeptical looks hadn't left their faces.

"I don't know how," countered Paige. "Years ago my neighborhood would have been all white Southerners, but today it looks like a mini United Nations. One family is from India, another from Korea. I know at least one from Africa, another from Germany, and one from Brazil. What kind of common ground could I use to reach them? Do you think there's a way I can use my home to reach such a diverse group?"

Brittany was the first to answer. "You could get Jim involved in helping you. That'll give you guys a common focus in your Christian outreach that can't help but be extra glue in an already good marriage."

Suzanne furrowed her brow, looking as if she was at least considering the possibilities. "Trying to reach our neighborhood sounds great," she said, "but I'm so busy at church. They've got me on just about every committee imaginable . . ." She paused, hearing the irony of what she'd just said. Brittany sensed it too and smiled at her friend.

"I know, I know," said Suzanne, nodding her agreement to the unspoken thought. "Too busy in the church to reach those outside it. Okay, tell me again how that birthday party thing would work."

Can Your Home Be a Nerve Center for Ministry?

This conversation could be repeated over and over across the land. Women from different circumstances in life want to make a difference and want their homes to be nerve centers for ministry. For too long life has been segmented into what we call *Time* magazine "lifestyles": business, community, sports, church, and so on. Segmentation and compartmentalization have overtaken too many followers of Christ and led them to think that the primary focus for ministry is the brick-and-mortar church building. But long before the church was created, God ordained the very first institution: the home. It should never be either/or. Ministry doesn't have to happen in one or the other; it should happen in both.

But if we're not careful, we can get so busy at church with multiple responsibilities that we don't have time to get to know our neighbors or to build bridges to them over which Jesus can cross from our lives to theirs.

What if, in addition to having one significant ministry in the church, all church members (just like Brittany, Paige, and Suzanne) were challenged to be missionaries to their neighborhoods, their kids' friends and parents, the people with whom they work, and those who may never enter the doors of a church on their own? These three fictitious friends are like so many women across the United States, those who work and those who stay at home. Many of those women have a deep desire to make their homes not only a nest and respite from the world but also a launching pad from which *to make a difference in the world.*

The question is, how is that possible, while still staying sane in today's hectic and busy culture?

MODERN ROLE MODELS

In today's world, June Cleaver (wife and mother on the old *Leave It to Beaver* television series, for those of you too young to remember!) is a woman of the past. And we're not sure she was ever a realistic role model. What June did best was say, "Yes, dear," or "Now be patient with the Beaver, dear." And she was always smiling at the door as

Ward left for work and when he came back home. Always in hose and heels, of course.

Today's woman has a personality of her own. She has skills and strengths, multiple talents and interests and a gifted mind. Her family means everything to her, and she wants to make a difference in her world as well. She may work inside the home, outside, or both. Gone are the days when one size fits all.

Whether a woman finds herself in the marketplace full-time or part-time or as a stay-at-home mom, how can she make her home a nerve center for ministry?

As we've been watching both stay-at-home moms and part-time or full-time workers, we've been amazed at the creativity of Christian women who find ways to make a difference without adding a lot of additional time commitments and activities to their already demanding schedules. We'll share a few of them to spark your imagination.

A BIRTHDAY PARTY FOR JESUS

A homemaker in Cumming, Georgia, Linda Ebert is an accomplished writer and editor who has been employed in the marketplace. She was on staff with Campus Crusade for Christ and Focus on the Family, but now her focus is on her four children. Linda and Mike realize they are growing like weeds. They range in age from four to eleven.

Linda knows God calls us to be *on mission* right where we are, so she began thinking how she might impact her neighborhood. Christmas was coming, and this gave her an idea. She knew that even families who rarely go to church are usually comfortable with Christmas traditions and may even long to go deeper into the "reason for the season" but don't have a clue how. Linda decided to have a birthday party for Jesus, which she thought could help fill this need and open some doors to substantive discussions with neighbors.

Linda and her kids worked together on the project, making

invitations and walking house to house to invite kids in their age range. As each mother came to the door, Linda explained that they were hand-delivering invitations to a very special birthday party for a very special Person.

Linda was careful not to hide the party's intent from the mothers. She knew this was an opportunity to develop open communication and trust. She explained specifically what their kids would be doing: celebrating the birth of the One whom Christmas is all about . . . singing songs about Jesus . . . enjoying a birthday cake . . . playing games such as Pin the Tail on Mary's Donkey . . . having an all-around blast! As the highlight, Linda would read the story of Jesus' birth from a book written in language children could understand about the birth of the greatest Person who ever lived.

Mother after mother was thrilled with the idea and excited about her children going to the party. Some mothers wanted to come too!

Linda involved her kids at every step. They transformed the kitchen into a party-favor factory and made goody bags for the children to take home. Linda gathered her kids around the table daily to pray for each invited child, emphasizing that the party's ultimate purpose was to let others know that God loved them so much that He sent His only Son to change their lives . . . and their parents' lives as well. Who knew what this holiday event might accomplish?

That first party was several years ago. Linda has continued hosting a birthday party for Jesus every year. The doors that have opened to share how Jesus can come into the heart of a child have also flung open to the parents who ask questions about this Jesus for whom the Eberts have such a special party.

And Linda is already planning an event for when her kids outgrow the Jesus birthday party. She's thinking of a party for preteen girls based on Josh McDowell's book *Why Wait?* which is geared to prepare each young lady with a biblical worldview of purity and its importance in life. The special presentation, yet to be completed, will focus on the topic "Why does true love wait?"

It's a Wonderful Life Party

Linda and her husband, Mike, wanted to reach out to their adult neighbors too—especially people who didn't regularly go to church. They looked for a creative way to use their own home, so people could experience the difference Christ makes in a marriage and a family.

They named the party after one of their favorite movies, *It's a Wonderful Life*. The first party was a big success, so now it's an annual event. Food and laughter are in abundance as they gather to watch the timeless Christmas classic starring Jimmy Stewart. During hors d'oeuvres, Mike leads the guests through a movie trivia contest; for example: "What's happening each time a bell rings?" (For the movie-challenged: the answer is that an angel gets his wings.) Everyone records his or her answers on cards provided by the Eberts. And some of the answers are a scream!

Then lights, camera, action . . .

While they have their guests' attention for the trivia contest, Mike shares briefly why the Ebert family has "a wonderful life." The answer, they explain, is simple: a personal relationship with Jesus Christ, a relationship anyone can have for the asking.

Over the years the Eberts discovered that the American Tract Society has created a tract based on the movie, explaining how to know Jesus Christ as Savior. Buying quantities of *It's a Wonderful Life* tracts every year, Mike and Linda place them in the hands of their guests as they leave, along with some home-baked Christmas goodies.

Needless to say, doors have flung open because this low-key, nonthreatening, home-based strategy is so successful for starting a conversation.

Remember the coffee klatch at Starbucks early in this chapter? Brittany and her husband could take a great page from Linda and Mike's playbook. Any couple could do this party without interrupting

their family life and schedule. Let's face it: once your house is deco-
rated for Christmas, you're dying to show it off anyway! And Costco,
Sam's Club, and BJ's are great places to find inexpensive, prepared
entertainment food! All it takes is a strong dose of intentionality, a
pinch of hospitality, and a healthy dash of prayerful anticipation.

CHANGING THE CULTURE OF
YOUR CHILD'S SCHOOL

Betsy Batchelor lived in coastal Virginia and was a volunteer at her
children's grade school. She had a ministry in her local church, but she
also was committed to making a difference in her children's lives—
and a big part of that was the school day. She noticed problems: the
increasing secularization of curriculum and the sad reality that public
schools do not focus on the values that were such a regular part of the
foundation of America. Betsy determined to make her life count by
investing in the culture of the school her kids attended.

In a day in which values-clarification courses were the hot topic
in teaching, Betsy discovered that some material being used was
devoid of our historic Judeo-Christian values and was liberal in its
leaning. But Betsy was convinced she could have some influence if
she invested time and help in the school with whatever needed to be
done. When the school counselor was considering what curriculum
to use, Betsy chimed in, "I'll be glad to help make available some of
the greatest values material I know of in America. It's called *McGee
and Me,* made especially for the school-age children you're teaching."

Betsy was familiar with the wonderful material used by Focus on
the Family. It zeroes in on building into children the biblically based
but nondenominational values that have made our nation great:
integrity, responsibility, standing by our promises, respecting the
rights of others, and serving those around us.

The school adopted Betsy's recommendation and throughout the
third, fourth, and fifth grades (eight hundred kids), *McGee and Me*

became the resource for values training—simply because one woman decided to make a difference in the normal traffic pattern of her life.

Betsy's role had a big impact on the Reccord family . . . but at first, we didn't even know it. Early one morning Betsy and Cheryl were power-walking through the neighborhood, huffing and puffing but talking at the same time. Cheryl commented that she had been concerned about the values-clarification course in the schools.

"Well," Cheryl almost shouted, trying to catch her breath, "you can just imagine how stunned I was when Ashley told me it was her favorite class. I went cold inside, but I asked her what they were teaching. And I about fell over when she said, 'Oh, Mom, it's great! We watch *McGee and Me!*' Betsy, can you believe that? That's material made for schools by Focus on the Family, and it's terrific! Can you believe it?"

With a twinkle in her eye and a new energy in her stride, Betsy just replied, "Oh, I can believe it!"

And our friends at Starbucks? Don't you think Suzanne, being a gifted judge, could come up with some creative ideas for material to teach kids at her daughter's school about the foundation of faith on which this country's legal system and government were founded? Organizations such as Wall Builders have researched the Judeo-Christian roots of America's heritage. While revisionist history conveniently leaves out the role of faith and values in our roots, parents like Suzanne could find creative ways to once again inject the real facts into the mainstream of education.

All it takes is thinking creatively, being concerned about what our kids are really learning, building a bridge to the school leadership, and earning a right to be heard.

Start Now!

Begin where you are in order to arrive where you want to be. To get a start on your direction, consider writing a mission statement on how to use your home to make a difference in the lives of others. Here are a few suggestions.

START BY KNOWING THE MISSION OF YOUR FAMILY'S LIFE

- What do you believe God has called you and your kids to do? Reach the family next door? Impact your school? Become known as the family neighbors can turn to if they have questions about the Bible or want to know more about God?

- Identify the gifts and talents that can help you make a difference as you use your home as a base. Did God provide you with a big backyard suitable for neighborhood barbecues? Do you enjoy company but hate to cook—yet love to use a credit card for takeout buffets? Are you a behind-the-scenes type, competent with a computer for putting together curriculum, but not one to speak to a group?

- How could your family work with you? What would be each person's role based on his or her personality, age, and interests? Realize this will be a personal growth opportunity for each child—and also for you as parents.

- Think of your family's mission statement as a legacy. Consider how you are modeling this principle for your children by being *on mission* with Him right where you are—starting now.

SCHEDULE A TIME TO PRAY AND PLAN

- Begin with prayer, asking God for wisdom and discernment so this will be a joyful opportunity rather than a burden.

- After the prayer, have a family meeting to brainstorm out-of-the-box ideas of how a ministry based from the home can make a difference in the lives of people who are already in your lives.

- List where your normal traffic pattern takes you, with home as "base camp." Does Dad often bring out-of-town guests home for dinner? Could you host an after-soccer hot-dog party for kids and parents? If your family already visits Grandma in her retirement community on a regular basis, could you turn this into a ministry opportunity?

- Solicit lots of input from even the youngest members of your family, emphasizing that there are no bad ideas. Review your list and narrow down the possibilities.

- Decide on an activity. List the steps that need to be done, making assignments that involve everyone in the family so each has a sense of ownership.

Set a Goal, and Make It Prominent

- It's easy to talk about the action plan; it's another thing to do it. Pray that God will help you take the first step in your action plan, so the family has a sense of teamwork and moving toward a successful goal.

- Write down your plan. Putting it in writing makes a dream concrete—more of a family contract.

- Make your action plan *doable, measurable, practical,* and *enjoyable.*

- Put your plan in a prominent place such as a refrigerator or mirror, or perhaps a sticky note on the dashboard of your car.

Stay on Track

- Commit to follow through and hold each other accountable on the accomplishment of the project.

- Remember that you'll be tempted to overestimate what

you can accomplish in a month and underestimate what you can accomplish in six to twelve months. So keep the end in mind and adjust your plan when necessary. It's important for this plan to be a success, not only to honor God, but to motivate your family to be *on mission*—right where they are.

- Make it fun. Every family project should be fun *and* devoted to building relationships that will lead to sharing Christ. It should be as enjoyable as possible, so everyone will cooperate.
- Celebrate as a family when you've accomplished your goal!

So what are you waiting for? Start coloring outside some lines!

CHAPTER 17

MEET PAM AND
MIKE STABILE

P am had a teaching position and Mike was blowing his coach's whistle one day when it dawned on him: *This isn't just a playing field—it's my mission field.*

He and Pam had struggled for years with the false notion that God could use them only if they went into professional ministry.

We kept denying the fact that God had enabled both of us to be educators. *That's only a vocation,* we thought, *not really the ministry.* I left teaching and went to Moody Bible Institute, feeling that God was leading me to be a pastor, which I was for nine years. But all along God was saying, "Wherever I plant you, that's where your ministry is." Finally, we realized teaching wasn't just our tent-making, a way to make money. He wanted us to have a voice in education, to discover a mission field we kept denying.

It was a freeing moment—a process, really—for two people who had taken their faith very seriously. Pam and Mike met in college while they were in Campus Crusade for Christ, then joined the staff of Crusade right after they married in 1977. "My goal was for Pam and me to be on campus and eventually for me to be a campus director," says Mike. "But God had different plans for us. And He has a way of putting you in places."

Yes, God calls you to be *on mission* with Him right where you are—starting now.

WINDOW MOMENTS

The Stabiles began praying for their daughters, even before they were born, that God would bring them to a saving relationship with Christ, that He would make them disciples and use them in the lives of people, fulfilling the Great Commission. "Since Pam and I are first-generation believers, in our hearts we had a desire to raise a new generation of lovers of God, who really want others to know Him."

Both grew up in what they call "negative environments." Their parents were loving, but they didn't know how to be transparent and real, could never show vulnerability, could never say they were sorry. "We wanted to start a generation that wasn't like that," says Mike. "We wanted to ask forgiveness and to humble ourselves before our children. We wanted to be purposeful about it."

But it wasn't easy. They tried family devotionals, but the kids were turned off, finding the lessons too predictable. So Pam and Mike took advantage of teachable moments in their kids' lives. Explains Pam:

> We call them "window moments," when they've had questions or when we can teach them biblical lessons based on something we heard or observed together, even times when they've made bad choices. We've seen window moments transform their lives. These

are still the most profitable times for us to provide direction to our kids, even though now they're all out of the nest.

And the result? Pam's answer may surprise you. "The most beautiful outcome of these window moments—such a natural habit of our lives—is that now our kids have become our greatest teachers. It's unbelievable how they can 'smell sin' in our lives. They challenge us. To some people that might sound invasive, but we welcome it."

As a result, Pam and Mike feel they've grown stronger as Christians. Explains Mike: "We've worked at being vulnerable, open, and transparent with our girls. I think we've grown in that. We recognize how at times we are stubborn as parents. And our own sin has caused problems. But we've allowed them to see our humanity and how we deal with it."

Ice-Cream Socials

The Stabiles warn their kids that "Christianity isn't a bed of roses." Pam says, "We don't try to paint them a picture that's unrealistic."

Adds Mike: "It's about being a disciple. The North American concept of Christianity is that it's all about fellowship and cookies and ice-cream socials. That's so inaccurate. We've got to prepare this generation for the hard stuff."

They quote 2 Timothy 3:12: "'In fact, everyone who wants to live a godly life in Christ Jesus will be persecuted.' Part of discipleship is recognizing that this life isn't easy. They need to expect it, and it's just part of following Christ." A tough message softened by Mike: "It's a joy. Jesus said you can still experience joy in spite of it all."

But Mike can deliver a tough message, and he's often called to do that in his mission field: a school in an affluent area.

I counsel so many parents. When their kids wind up in the principal's office and the parents object, I start asking questions. I usually find the problem is their parenting style. Too often they've lost the concept of being a parent. They want to be their children's friend. The parents don't want their kids not to like them, so they back down when their kids say: "I hate you. Why are you doing this to me?"

What the parents should respond is: "Okay, you may hate me now, but I'm your parent, not your friend, and I have to set boundaries for you. It's for your own good, and it's because I love you." I've shared that with so many parents. Some take the advice, and some don't. The ones who continue in the old way are paying the consequences for their kids' lives. Issue after issue keeps coming up for those families, and you see it in the attitudes and actions of the kids.

Mike stresses that parents (and educators) can't take all responsibility away from the children and lay it at the feet of the parents. But in raising his own, he focused less on their behavior and more on their character and attitude, the root causes. "We've observed parents who have focused too much on the outward appearances of their children, and now they're reaping the effects of that."

We'll close with other insights from the Stabiles:

Mike: Our first mentors were Delmas and Marta Jones, godly believers who let us observe their family in action. The neat thing is they didn't just say, "Here's what you need to do." Instead, they invited us to spend time with their family, especially at the dinner table. We saw how they made family times natural, how everybody had a voice in talking. Nobody ever left the table. Pam and I weren't accustomed to that while we were growing up. We had family meals, but we didn't really communicate with each other. This family really explored topics, the sacred and the secular. They practiced the Hebrew relational model of living life with their kids.

Pam: We encourage our girls to always put themselves in situations where they're accountable to someone who has walked with the Lord a little longer, [who is] a bit more mature. It's also a way to keep them communicating about matters of faith, talking heart to heart. A few years ago we had an incident with our middle daughter coming home for the summer. Our oldest challenged her to share her heart with us. It turned out to be very painful for us to hear. She said she felt insecure and threatened. But it was good to get it on the table and just ask each other's forgiveness and hold each other. Our family life has never been the same.

Pam: This is such a liberal, affluent community [Ohio]. Parents buy alcohol for the kids to serve at their parties. The parking lot at school is full of fancy cars, and they belong to the kids, not the teachers. By the time teens are freshmen or sophomores in high school, dances are such old hat that they have coed sleepovers. Most kids have had sex by that time. So when our girls turned thirteen, we had open discussions about the purity issue, saving themselves for their husbands, and then we gave them either a ring or a necklace to signify their commitment. Yet even in this environment, when our youngest daughter was sixteen, she led a Bible study on purity, taking a countercultural stand with strength and confidence.

Mike: We have an expression in our family: "Go mad. Make a difference." It's our way of reminding each other that God called us, and we can't wait for a better time or place to serve Him. We do it here and now.

CHAPTER 18

WHAT'S YOUR JOB?

PRINCIPLE 5

God reveals His mission through His Word, His Spirit, wise counsel, and His work in circumstances around you.

Key Scriptures

His Word—All Scripture is God-breathed and is useful for teaching, rebuking, correcting and training in righteousness, so that the man of God may be thoroughly equipped for every good work. (2 Timothy 3:16–17)

His Spirit—But when he, the Spirit of truth, comes, he will guide you into all truth. He will not speak on his own; he will speak only what he hears, and he will tell you what is yet to come. (John 16:13)

Wise counsel—Plans fail for lack of counsel, but with many advisers they succeed. (Proverbs 15:22)

His work—God knew what he was doing from the very beginning. He decided from the outset to shape the lives of those who love him along the same lines as the life of his Son. The Son stands first in the line of humanity he restored. We see the original and intended shape of our lives there in him. After God made that decision of what his children should be like, he followed it up by calling people by name. After he called them by name, he set them on a solid basis with himself. And then, after getting them established, he stayed with them to the end, gloriously completing what he had begun. (Romans 8:29–30 MSG)

Let's get real. What's the primary responsibility we have as parents, anyway?

To make our kids happy, right? To give them everything they need (because they'd never admit it's just a want)? To keep them from all disappointments? To discipline? While that list may sound appealing, it's not biblical. What God really wants of us as parents is to provide an environment for our children where they can grow increasingly mature, so they can make biblically based decisions that allow them to become everything He created them to be.

That means we have to help our kids learn the ways of God, and not just the ways of society—for often they are diametrically opposed. Let's go back to that vital verse of Scripture in Proverbs 22:6: "Train a child in the way he should go, / and when he is old he will not turn from it." Some people say this means teaching our children in the ways of God. Others claim it addresses the need to learn how He wired our kids, personality- and temperament-wise. Both views actually bear great truth.

To accomplish Proverbs 22:6, we as parents must make sure *we* understand what the Owner's Manual (God's Word) teaches about godly decision making . . . *and* that we're doing it ourselves. So one thing we hope this chapter will do is encourage you to perform a quick checkup on your own life to see how you're doing according to God's design for decision making. Because ultimately, your job is to role-model this principle, which is always the best way to teach, isn't it?

KNOWING LIFE'S PLAYBOOK IN ORDER TO CALL THE RIGHT PLAYS

God has always used four primary means to reveal His mission and calling for our lives. They haven't changed, and they never will. So as parents we need to make sure, to the best of our ability, that we have modeled for our kids all four to help them understand

1. The importance of God's Word in decision making
2. The importance of God's Holy Spirit in decision making
3. The importance of wise counsel in decision making
4. The importance of God's work in the circumstances around our lives in decision making

In the early years of our marriage, we had the privilege of living in Dallas, Texas—home of the Cowboys. Dubbed by fans and sports-writers as "America's football team," the Cowboys were at the top of their game, winning championships and Super Bowls, and Coach Tom Landry (a committed Christian) was often in the news. Even opponents admired him, and reporters met his flights in hopes of a quote. Once, after another victory, Coach Landry emerged from the plane with his wife's hand in one of his and a book of some kind in the other. A reporter asked what it was. "This is the playbook for my life," answered Landry, holding up his well-worn Bible.

It can't be said any better than that! Just as a football team has a playbook that guides its decision making on the field, so God gave us a playbook to guide our decision making in life. After all, that's why we have cookbooks: to guide us to use the right ingredients at the right time to come out with the right results.

And that's what God said about the Word He gave us and its purpose. In 2 Timothy 3:16–17, God made it clear that there were four primary reasons He gave His Word to us:

1. To teach us the right way to live and the right decisions to make

2. To cause us discomfort when we're not living and deciding that way

3. To show us how to get back on the right track in our living and decision making

4. To show us how to stay on the right track

After all, God wants us to succeed. God told Joshua as the Hebrews went in to conquer the Promised Land that Joshua's decisions would be absolutely essential to their victory, and good decisions demanded his faithfulness to Scripture.

> Be strong and very courageous. Be careful to obey all the law my servant Moses gave you; do not turn from it to the right or to the left, that you may be successful wherever you go. Do not let this Book of the Law depart from your mouth; meditate on it day and night, so that you may be careful to do everything written in it. *Then* [and only then] *you will be prosperous and successful.* (Joshua 1:7–8, italics ours)

Did you grab that? *God wants us—and our kids—to be successful.* That passage in the original language refers to making wise decisions. And the principles of His Book will help us to do that better than anything else in existence. For Joshua, in conquering the Promised Land, God's Word was to be the field book for decisions that would bring victory.

If you turn back just a couple of pages in Scripture, you'll find that God, at the close of Moses' life, had made clear to Joshua that the Word wasn't simply a good book, but something far more important: "Take to heart all the words I have solemnly declared to you this day, so that you may command your children to obey carefully *all* the words of this law. They are not just idle words for you—*they are your life*" (Deut. 32:46–47, italics ours).

God said that His Word is not just the *basis* for good decision making in life; *it is the very essence of life.*

King David told us over and over how important he found the Word of God. Just listen:

> The law of the LORD is perfect,
>   reviving the soul.
> The statutes of the LORD are trustworthy,
>   making wise the simple.
> The precepts of the LORD are right,
>   giving joy to the heart.
> The commands of the LORD are radiant,
>   giving life to the eyes.
> The fear of the LORD is pure,
>   enduring forever.
> The ordinances of the LORD are sure
>   and altogether righteous.
> They are more precious than gold,
>   than much pure gold;
> They are sweeter than honey,
>   than honey from the comb.
> By them is your servant warned;
>   in keeping them there is great reward. (Psalm 19:7–11)

Take a moment and go through these one by one, writing in the margin what they mean as they characterize God's Word—especially what they personally mean to you and your child. For example, in the margin next to "The law of the LORD is perfect, / reviving the soul," you might write, "The Bible contains all we need for revival."

Now take a moment and read through Psalm 119, marking every time it says something about the importance of God's Word. Look for key words such as "laws," "commands," "precepts," "statutes," "decrees," "promises," "ways."

And note what the psalmist said about his focus on the importance of God's Word: "My heart is set on keeping your decrees / *to the very end*" (Ps. 119:112, italics ours).

If you don't do anything for your kids other than help them know how to use the Bible as life's playbook, you will have achieved a great success and left an awesome legacy. Before you read any further, why don't you make a plan to share with your children, at their levels and in their language, what you've discovered (or been reminded of) about the importance of God's Word? Don't ever underestimate what it will mean for your kids to hear it directly from you.

And be sure you're attending a church where they're regularly hearing it from their pastor and teachers. Inspirational talks aren't enough in these days to help our kids safely navigate the rapid currents of their lives. They desperately need to be in a church where all the leadership regularly talk about God's Word and demonstrate how they apply it in their own lives.

EVERY TIME I FEEL THE SPIRIT MOVING IN MY HEART, I WILL PRAY

These words are from a spiritual entitled "Every Time I Feel the Spirit," and they're a great testimony of the writer's understanding of the Holy Spirit. Jesus promised that when He ascended back into heaven following His resurrection, He would send His Holy Spirit to guide us in our lives. In John 16, which records Jesus' time with the disciples before the Crucifixion, He made clear that when He was taken from them, God would send the Holy Sprit as an internal compass and navigation system for how to walk in the right way.

Sometimes it's difficult for our kids to comprehend how the Holy Spirit works in our lives. Here are two examples you can use to explain how much God loves them by providing the Holy Spirit for them and their daily decision making.

A Navigation System

If you have a vehicle with an OnStar navigation system, you've found how amazing it is. If not, maybe you can rent a car that has one in it. It will blow your mind!

You can literally be anywhere in your car, push the OnStar navigation button, and hear a representative respond and ask how he or she can help. When you say what you need, the rep will find out the answer, whether it's directions or arrangements, to get you where you need to go.

We heard of a man who was traveling in his new Cadillac and a light kept coming on on his dashboard. He called OnStar, and the rep asked him to please be patient while he checked all his systems by satellite computer. When the rep came back on, he informed the driver that he had found no difficulty traceable by satellite transmission from all the computers in his car; however, his right rear tire was about eight pounds low! Can you believe that?

That's not all. OnStar had called the nearest dealership a couple of miles ahead and made arrangements for him to stop in quickly just to double-check that light on the dash. Then the OnStar rep added that the service manager would be waiting for him with a smile!

We were stunned. But guess what's even more amazing: the fact that God has given us the Holy Spirit, once we accept Jesus as Savior, to be the best navigation system we could ever have.

A WARNING SYSTEM

But the Holy Spirit is not just a navigation system; He's also a warning system. Another example you can use with your kids is the invisible fence some people install in their yards to keep their pets from wandering. We've mentioned that we have one for our dog, Abbey. Abbey will go only to the boundary of the invisible fence and no farther because of the electronic collar she wears.

Here's how we trained her. We held her electronic collar in one hand and her on a short leash in the other while we walked her to the boundary installed at the edge of our yard. As we approached it, the collar started to beep; then we turned to Abbey and said firmly, "No, no, no!" After a few days of training, she learned that beyond that line was a territory to avoid.

In a similar way, God's Holy Spirit comes to reside in the lives of our kids once they have personally received Jesus Christ as Savior. From that point on, part of His role is to warn them not to go in certain directions. That warning can be for their safety, to keep them from mistakes, or to lead them to an even more fruitful and productive opportunity.

Read Acts 16, which records that the Holy Spirit cautioned Paul not to go one way, but to go another. Was the direction he was headed wrong? Not necessarily. But the direction God's Holy Spirit prompted him to go instead opened up Europe to the gospel! Not a bad prompt, don't you agree?

Your desire for your children to understand this principle never stops. Our twenty-eight-year-old single daughter, Christy, had her job come to a sudden and abrupt halt when the company representative walked in one day and said to everyone gathered, "We're shutting down the organization. It just hasn't made enough money, so we're going to cut our losses and move forward. Therefore, all of you will be without a job." That really made her day!

And ours too, come to think of it. So we have prayerfully, and with a lot of concern, been walking with our daughter through a decision-making process about a new job.

After looking at multiple opportunities, and considering our hopes that she might come back closer to Atlanta, she finally sensed a clear leading to the other side of the world: namely, San Diego. (When you're a parent, that seems like the other side of the world!) Christy is moving as we write this very chapter, and our pride in her is enormous, because we've watched her decision-making process: she's prayed regularly, she's asked the right questions of advisers, she's sought counsel in His Word, and she's been sensitive to the prompting of the Holy Spirit as to which step was best. We are thrilled with her awareness that God's Holy Spirit serves as the OnStar navigation system for the issues of her life.

COUNSEL FROM THOSE WHO HAVE BEEN THERE

Take a minute and ask yourself a question: *where do I get my advice?*

Dr. Phil? How about Oprah? *Redbook* or *Cosmopolitan*? Or maybe *Men's Health* or *USA Today*? Or maybe from shows such as *Renovate My Family* on Fox, *My Wife and Kids,* or the syndications of *Seinfeld?* Okay, we're kidding. But maybe your source is a little bit closer to you, such as a fellow parent who isn't much farther along on the journey of parenting than you are.

God has built into our lives the capacity to gather and assimilate wise counsel from others. David got it from Nathan, Moses got it from Jethro, Pharaoh got it from Joseph, and the early church received it from such leaders as Peter and Paul.

The key is choosing good advice givers. Parents must help their children learn to choose wisely the people who influence them. One of the best ways to accomplish that is to share with your kids how you select people from whom you receive counsel. Consider the following:

- What qualities do you look for?
- How do you determine their levels of wisdom?
- How do you determine their track record of decision making?
- How do you know they are good, Bible-based decision makers as opposed to just clever thinkers?

We encourage you to invite people into your home whom you greatly respect for their biblical decision making. Let your kids see them up close. Provide opportunities where your kids can talk with them or sit around the table during meals and listen to them (but remember, kids don't want to just listen, *they want to engage*!). It's amazing what our kids absorb even when they aren't in the spotlight of carrying the conversation.

We have been fortunate to have people such as Bill and Vonette Bright, Henry and Marilyn Blackaby, and Jay and Diane Strack, as well as other wonderful Christian leaders, in our home. But every bit as important have been less-well-known people with career specializations and hearts for the Lord: Steve Sanford, a media and computer expert deeply committed to using these technologies for the kingdom, and his wife, Kim; Jeff McWaters, who works in the healthcare industry, and his wife, Cindy; and accountant Carlos Ferrer and his wife, Cindy, who is a nurse. All of these people have touched our kids in different ways at different times as they have fleshed out their walks with Christ in biblically based decisions.

And one of the things we've both tried to do is consistently tell our kids the stories of different friends who have gone through excellent biblical decision making in which Jesus has come out the hero of their story. That's very important, because the hero in biblically based decision making is never the individual person, but always Jesus as the One who led them to the right decision. That is a critical concept, in our belief, to get across to our kids for their own decision-making process.

SEEKING GOD'S HAND AND TRUSTING GOD'S HEART

Imagine these scenarios: Your child wants an opportunity so much (to be chosen for the team, to be awarded the scholarship) but is passed over. Or your child feels rejected by the cool group at school (the cheerleading squad). Or some unforeseen circumstance changes your child's future plans (the family moves to another town). As a parent, how do you counsel a child when hopes are dashed—but unexpected pathways open up before him?

Helping our kids see God at work in the disappointing times as well as the affirming and exhilarating times is a crucial role for parents. It's one of our greatest tests and challenges. And it's a critical lesson for children to learn, because as they fulfill the missions God has for them, repeatedly they will experience disappointments, times of defeat, huge challenges, and blindsides. But here's a warning: if they are to navigate successfully the mission God has for them, we must help them avoid the victim mentality when things go wrong. Frankly, kids pick up a lot of their cues about handling tough times from their parents, whether we want to admit it or not. For example, how many times have you heard parents say things like:

> My daughter didn't make the cheerleading squad, because the tryouts weren't fair. They were rigged to favor the beautiful girls and not focused on the talent and skill of every girl. That's why she didn't make it.

> My son wasn't elected class officer because he ran his campaign fairly, but his opponent did everything short of bribing kids to vote for him. If my son had stooped to such low tactics, he would have won it hands-down.

I can't trust the coach, because he almost never puts my kid in the game. A lot of people have told me that my kid is one of the best players on the field, but for whatever reason the coach just has something against my kid. It's unfair!

These all have one thing in common: they make the child into a victim. And the child picks up on that attitude and runs with it to an extreme.

What if the parents had chosen instead to talk about what God is teaching their children in a disappointing set of circumstances? What if they had pointed out to their children opportunities to grow and rebound from what could have been interpreted as failure? And what if they'd helped their children understand that all through life will be times when we cannot clearly see or understand God's hand—but we can *always* trust His heart?

Parents who unwittingly position their children as victims are really trying to help build up their kids, but in reality the opposite is happening. They're offering a built-in "excuse legacy" that the child will perfect and strengthen with each passing year, preventing him from taking responsibility for his own growth, deepening his faith, or stepping on the face of disappointment as an overcomer. Our role as parents is not to protect our children by always making them feel that they're right, no matter what. Instead we must help them discern with wisdom the circumstances before them and search for God's hand, or at least His heart, in the midst of disappointment.

When we moved to Georgia, our son was two months short of eighteen. He had just finished his junior year in high school in Virginia and had been president of his class, was on the football and golf teams, and was . . . well, an all-around BMOC (big man on campus).

We had included him in the decision about moving to Atlanta, getting his perspective and insight, as we had the other two kids. We didn't force anything on anybody, and Bryan had even said he knew

God's will was that we should move to Atlanta for the professional opportunity that had been presented to Bob.

But in reality, by the time we got to Atlanta, Bryan had a chip on his shoulder the size of Gibraltar (which he freely admits these days at twenty-five years of age).

We tried to help him see how God was opening doors of opportunity for him. He had done well enough in high school that after three years, he had only a few credits left to complete to graduate, and so he finished high school in three and a half years. Next, although he was young, after moving to Atlanta he had an amazing opportunity to travel the country to help set up a national student conference. This took him to cities such as Orlando, Dallas, and San Diego. He was the only eighteen-year-old we knew who was paid to travel the country, stay in wonderful hotels with king-size beds, and gain the experience of setting up a major national conference. But even though he did an excellent job with his work, the chip remained immovable.

Now, several years later, he can see how the change in his life laid the groundwork for his present job, which has aspects of responsibility literally around the world. And it gave him the added courage that prompted him two years later to go to Germany for the summer, where he knew no one, to study the German language, so he could become fluent in a world-respected tongue.

Today he's married, has an excellent job where he's been commended repeatedly for his effectiveness, and admits that God's hand was preparing him for his future. And here's what we want to convey to you: there were many times, as we tried to help him see God's hand, or at least trust God's heart, when we felt like failures. The chip remained. The moodiness continued. The shortness with his two sisters was exacerbated, and life at home was tense.

But through it we learned some important lessons as parents.

- We are not responsible for our children's responses when we try to teach them biblical truths. We are simply responsible as parents to be consistent in attempting to teach to our children the truth that God has unique plans and callings for missions in their lives that are bigger than they are.

- We as parents also need to learn to trust God's heart when we can't see His hand, even in dealing with our kids! Because given time, they'll remember how we dealt with these issues beyond our control.

- We also are responsible for helping our kids give God the credit He rightfully deserves when things go well. If they're not careful, it's easy for our kids (and us!) to grab the credit and mentally leave God standing in the corner alone.

Today, we're still trying to encourage and remind our kids that in every situation, they can trust God's heart, even if they can't immediately see His hand at work. Today, we're still stretching and learning as our kids continue to discover God's will and missions for their lives. And what a journey each of the three is having! But thankfully, so are we.

CHAPTER 19

MEET TRACEY AND MIKE PARROTT

Our fifth principle is *God reveals His mission through His Word, His Spirit, wise counsel, and His work in circumstances around you.* A family of six named the Parrotts embody this beautifully. And the reason is simple: each family member is a mature Christian with ministries of his or her own, each is learned about the Bible and capable of quoting and applying passages, yet each still relies daily on all four of these resources for guidance. The Parrotts have never outgrown their reliance on God. And they've never even slowed down in seeking His mission for their lives. What are their secrets?

Tracey has always participated in a women's study and support group, such as Moms in Touch. Meeting regularly with people in her stage in life, whatever that might be, keeps her sharp, focused, and challenged. She benefits from mentoring and being mentored. And she recognizes that such a group provides her with all four of the resources in this principle.

> I think it's vitally important for parents to pray, not only personally, but to pray with a small group for the lives and safety and spiritual growth of their children. I committed to pray one hour a week with these other moms all through the kids' elementary and high-school years. I felt that intentional commitment on my part with other moms to pray for our children and their school and their teachers was dramatically important in keeping them safe, covering them with protection.

Mike keeps a detailed prayer journal. During his children's growing-up years, he kept a separate page for each of four areas.

> One was vision for their lives. I was always praying for what God was going to envision, of how He might use them or how each is unique and able to sense God's leading in his or her life. The other three areas were conviction, character, and conduct. I prayed intentionally and deliberately through each area. Then I noticed how God was changing all four children in those areas. I made notations of the changes as a way to thank God and for encouragement as I observed their growth. It was important for us to notice how God was unfolding His plans for each of them.

As a couple, Mike and Tracey looked to their pastor and his wife as their personal mentors. This says a lot about Mike and Tracey, because they are in ministry too. But finding strong people to learn from and be accountable to has built them spiritually. Mike and Tracey have discovered mentors "don't just happen"—they have to be sought out and asked. But people who want to grow look for people who are a few steps ahead of them, people who can help them strengthen and improve their journeys. And nothing teaches kids the value of a mentor like seeing their parents have one!

The result for this family? All of the children have *on mission* lifestyles: making prayer and Bible study a regular part of their lives, seeking God's will for their futures, sharing Christ's sacrifice with their friends, seeking mission fields across the street or far from home. One by one they've traveled to such exotic places as Russia, Kenya, Macedonia, Hungary, and the Netherlands. Yet they also see public schools as mission fields. They lead student Bible studies and mentor young people who are newer Christians. They participate in ministries such as See You at the Pole (a day in September when high-school students gather at the flagpole to pray for their school and commit the year to God) and Campus Crusade. The four kids in this family have a true Acts 1:8 vision for reaching lost people.

WEEKLY DEVOTIONS

So by now you envision a house full of perfect kids and a family with daily meditations where everyone is intensively involved, right?

Wrong. Instead of trying to kill themselves with a devotion every day, the Parrotts were more realistic about their family's lifestyle. They participated in a once-a-week family time together around Bible study, followed by a game and prayer time, kneeling around the bed. When the kids were younger, Mike and Tracey read a Bible story. As the children got older, the parents gave them the opportunity to prepare and lead the study, using whatever materials they chose. This helped them develop creativity and leadership. They found the best night for their family to share this time together was Sunday.

And as for perfect kids, wrong again. Says Tracey:

Each has gone through things that we've had to deal with. One had a lying problem, and we had to really deal with that area and pray through it. One stole something from a store once, a simple pack of gum, but the consequences of that were taking it back, apologizing, and paying for it. As areas came up in their lives, we would intentionally focus on what was behind each one, what was going on. We didn't have legalistic rules that they had to live under, but issues came up that we felt would be detrimental to their growth.

I noticed that one of the kids was listening to a lot of secular music on the radio. It seemed odd, because we always had Christian CDs and the Christian radio station going. Rather than specifically ban the secular music, we took that as a clue that something was going on and used it as a point for dialogue.

Adds Mike:

Sometimes their language wasn't appropriate or what they were saying to another member of the family wasn't encouraging. Certain words weren't acceptable. They couldn't call each other "stupid." They couldn't say, "I hate you." Finally, after one of these breaches, I gave an assignment to one of the children: "Because of what you've said, you have to memorize Ephesians 4:29, and don't come right back. You're not done with this until you can say it from memory and explain to me what it means." So I held them accountable. Eventually all of them had to memorize that verse at some point.

We'll close with more of their ideas and wisdom:

Mike: In the last couple of graduations from high school, I asked each to give me a contemporary Christian song that was his or her favorite. We made videos of their lives to the background of those songs to encourage them how they'd grown not only physically but also spiritually. This became my graduation gift.

Tracey: My advice to parents who are just starting on the path of launching their kids with an *on mission* lifestyle—even though the kids may be halfway grown by now—is quite personal. I think you need to start with your own walk with God and make sure you are growing through Bible study, prayer, and being in an accountability group with mature Christians who can help you discern the circumstances in your life where God is at work. This will help you launch your children more than anything.

Mike: The key to our success is the fact that Tracey and I have been on target together. But that's taken effort.

CHAPTER 20

CROSSROADS OF CHOICE

PRINCIPLE 6

God will repeatedly bring you to crossroads of choice as He forges you for His mission.

Key Scriptures

> Now fear the LORD and serve him with all faithfulness . . . But if serving the LORD seems undesirable to you, then choose for yourselves this day whom you will serve . . . But as for me and my household, we will serve the LORD. (Joshua 24:14–15)

> But Daniel resolved not to defile himself with the royal food and wine, and he asked the chief official for permission not to defile himself this way. (Daniel 1:8)

189

> For we are God's workmanship [*poiema*, or masterpiece], created in Christ Jesus to do good works, which God prepared in advance for us to do. (Ephesians 2:10)

When we begin to make our own choices, it's a sure sign of maturity. For good or for bad, after a certain age, we all make our choices and live with the consequences. The most important choice we can ever help our kids make is what they will do with Jesus Christ. We emphasize in this book that no one—parents, grandparents, teachers, pastors—can make that decision for them. It's why Romans 10:9–10, which we quoted earlier, is so critically important: "If you confess with your mouth, 'Jesus is Lord,' and believe in your heart that God raised him from the dead, you will be saved. For it is with your heart that you believe and are justified, and it is with your mouth that you confess and are saved."

Take a minute, grab a pen, and circle each time the personal pronoun "you" or "your" is used. It drives home the fact that each person is responsible for *his or her own decision* as to what to do with the question of Jesus. Who do we say that He is? Will we recognize Him as Lord of our lives? Or will we stay in the driver's seat, in effect, declaring ourselves to be Lord instead of Him?

For those who relinquish control, a time comes to make a decision to invite Christ to be our Savior (forgiving our pasts) and Lord of our future (directing our every step). And that's when the miracle of grace occurs, because our salvation is not anything we can earn by how good we are or by the impressive list of good deeds we accomplish. Instead, it's a gift from God, given to us by Him as an act of pure grace, free for us to choose or reject: "For it is by grace you have been saved, through faith—and this not from yourselves, it is the gift of God—not by works, so that no one can boast" (Eph. 2:8–9).

Notice the words "this not from yourselves," and be reminded that the word "this" refers to both the act of grace and the gift of salvation—the whole package is a gift from God, and it's not based on our own efforts or good works. But don't lose sight of the fact that Ephesians 2:10 comes immediately on its heels: "For we are God's workmanship, created in Christ Jesus to do good works, which God prepared in advance for us to do." You may say it like this: my life has purpose, and God saved me for the work (mission) that He prepared especially for me.

CUMULATIVE CHOICES LEAD TO PATTERNS OF CHOOSING

We try to work out in an effort to stay in respectable shape. In these days of extreme makeovers, we've found it's a lot less expensive to take care of ourselves physically and work like mad through exercise in our war against the Battle of the Bulge.

Our workouts have taught us an important principle about the human muscle: repetition produces what the experts call "muscle memory." Athletes are familiar with it. Astronauts train over and over again to cultivate it. Special forces soldiers are experts at it.

The process builds on consistent choices. When someone chooses an action and practices it repeatedly, a "memory system" develops within his body. Done enough, the activity, motion, or action becomes second nature. People in certain professions (think of an astronaut whose control systems suddenly fail) know that in the heat of crisis, unexpected circumstances, the pressure of expectations, and rapidly changing conditions, the ability to act by second nature is absolutely essential. Also, exercise experts know that through repeating well-executed exercises, muscles begin to strengthen and build. In fact, those skilled and practiced in the physical sciences tell us that when someone repeatedly does choice exercise patterns in physical training, a whole subset of vessels begins to develop to augment the main vessels, arteries, and veins of the body. This explains why there come points in an exercise program when results plateau, followed by what seems like an explosion to another level—but only after consistent work. That's because the new augmenting vessels forming under the skin suddenly are like a new freeway that's been opened for the flow of blood and oxygen, which allows the person exercising to advance to new levels.

God, being the great Designer, wired our intellect in much the same way He wired us physically. We learn to make good choices by making good choices. We build a successful effort on top of a previous successful effort. One good decision builds on another. And when we make a bad decision, the consequences speak for themselves, and we are faced with the challenge to reconsider, retool, and redirect our actions and attitudes.

So just as a physical trainer can help us build our physical prowess, strengthen our coordination, and enhance our flexibility, we as parents are charged with responsibility for helping our kids develop their decision-making abilities. We become their spiritual trainers.

We have worked with several trainers, each with a different personality and style—everyone from Attila the Hun to Mr. Rogers. But one thing they all said to us is this: "I can show you what to do, I can demonstrate to you how to do it, and I can watch you as you practice. But week in and week out, the choice is going to be yours. I can't make you exercise or want to. You've got to make that choice for yourself. But the results will tell the story."

How very similar to the role we find ourselves in with our kids as they mature through the stages of their growth. While we can start out being very directive and present as they grow, increasingly we become the coaches and they become more responsible for the decisions they make (or don't make) and the consequences that result.

Great News from the Head Coach

It's true that parents must impress on children the serious responsibility of making good choices, but along the way we recommend adding healthy doses of encouragement and good news. And there's no better news than this: *God wants us to succeed in our choices!* God told Joshua that if he made his choices according to the Word of God, the choices would be wise and productive ones (Josh. 1:8). Even right choices, however, have consequences; sometimes they cost us in areas such as comfort, or they turn out to be a challenge for us to carry out. Yet they'll always be productive, and God will honor the choice made in line with His guidance and Word.

It's amazing how easy it is to get sucked into thinking that God is reluctant to give blessings to those who choose His way. We admit that sometimes even *we* find ourselves reflecting this perspective— not intentionally, of course. It's great that friends such as Beth Moore remind us with such encouraging words:

> God's willingness and unwavering desire to bless His people is one of the most repetitive concepts in both Testaments of His Word. He is the giver of all good gifts and greatly exults when a child cooperates enough to receive some. New Testament believers were promised blessing for obedience as surely as the children of God in the Old Testament.[1]

Beth adds: "Blessing is defined by neither ease nor worldly possessions nor stock-market successes. Blessing is bowing down to receive the expressions of divine favor that in the inner recesses of the human heart and mind make life worth the bother."[2]

God repeatedly told His people in the Old Testament that He was taking them into a life of blessing. Take a minute to read Deuteronomy chapters 8 and 30 just to be reminded how much God wanted to bless those who chose according to His will. And then jump to the New Testament and read Ephesians 1:3: "Praise be to the God and Father of our Lord Jesus Christ, who has blessed us in the heavenly realms with every spiritual blessing in Christ." Now answer:

- What has He done for you and your child?
- How many spiritual blessings has He made available?
- Whom do the blessings come through?

And how about the amazing promise of 2 Peter 1:3 (notice the 1:3, which will make both of these verses easy to remember)? There God declares: "His divine power has given us everything we need for life and godliness."

- How much has He given us and our children?
- What do you and your child need just for daily living?
- What do you need for godly living?

The parallels of Scripture are amazing: these two New Testament verses beautifully tie in with Joshua 1:3 (another 1:3!), where God told His people: "I will give you *every place* where you set your foot, as I promised" (italics ours). God has been a giving God. God *is* a giving God. And God always will be a giving God. It's critical that we help our kids understand that's the kind of God we're calling them to follow!

So how do we best help our kids understand the importance of solid, biblically based choices in their lives? We recommend introducing them to the heroes of Scripture who had to make life-impacting decisions early in their lives. In addition to biblical passages, find biographies of these people at your bookstore or on-line. Many are written with a young readership in mind. Here are several Bible characters and the principles of choice their stories illustrate:

- Joseph and the brothers who betrayed him—the choice of forgiving when forgiving is hard to do (Gen. 37–45)

- David and Goliath—the choice to stand up and be counted when God instructs us, even in the face of overwhelming odds (1 Sam. 17)

- Daniel, Shadrach, Meshach, and Abednego—the choice of standing by our convictions and beliefs in the midst of a radically opposing culture; never compromising to "fit in" (Dan. 1 and 3)

Each story brilliantly depicts a follower of God faced with a critical choice and the ramifications of the choices each made. Our kids need to learn that our choices don't affect just us; they affect everybody around us. And each choice requires a God-sized faith. A belief that

God is who He says He is,
He has the power that He says He has,
He can do what He says He can, and
He will reward what He promises to reward.

We love what our friend Henry Blackaby says about faith in his groundbreaking book *Experiencing God:* "Faith [is] believing that the God who called us to the assignments was the One who would provide for their accomplishment."[3]

Therefore, we as parents must remember (and share with our kids) that when it comes to pleasing God, faith is a must at the crossroads of choice. Hebrews 11:6 says, "Without faith it is *impossible* to please God" (italics ours).

And remember, faith that leads to action requires us to align our lives with the ways of God. We can't live out faith in our choices if areas of our lives are out of alignment with what God's Word says. This is true with parents, and it's true with kids. Are you or your children out of alignment in any of these areas?

Our attitudes: a rebellious heart, an undisciplined spirit, a desire to be our own boss, a resistance to accountability

Our relationships: close friendships with people who aren't Christ-followers, ruptured relationships with family members, lack of forgiveness

Our commitments: nonactive participation in a local church, not carrying out the things we promised to do, not being faithful to friends and family

Our actions: our language, our lack of a heart of servanthood, our resistance to giving, and our hurtful actions toward others' feelings

If areas such as these are out of alignment with what God clearly says, then we can't practice faith even if we want to. And the question of obedience to what God's Word says is not even on the radar screen of our lives. How can it be when these things are out of line? So, first, there must be an alignment before there can ever be a faithful obedience.

And when we make godly choices at the crossroads of our lives, or teach our children to do the same, we show what we really believe about God by the choices we make—no matter what we say!

FROM LEBANON TO GEORGIA

Rosalyn is the daughter of our good friends Randy and Rhonda Singer. After graduating from high school in Atlanta, she took off to California to attend Azusa Pacific University as a freshman. It was a new set of friends, a new state, and a new step in her life . . . and the farthest away she had ever been from her parents and brother on a continuous basis.

The year went great, but Rosalyn decided she wanted to spend the remainder of her college years closer to family and friends. When she applied to the University of Georgia, she expected to have little difficulty being admitted as an in-state resident with good grades from high school and a year of college under her belt. But to her shock and surprise, she was not accepted. Because of the large number of students that year, the university had to limit its acceptance of students such as Rosalyn who were applying to transfer from other colleges.

So Rosalyn stood at a crossroads of choice. What would she do? Get mad? Maybe God was just against her, and she got dealt the short end of the stick when it came to attaining her desires. Or maybe she would just sit around and do nothing until she could try again. Or maybe she would stay at Azusa Pacific, even though she didn't feel that was where she needed to be.

That was when faith came into the picture. Because of how her family dealt with crossroads of choice, anger was not even a temptation for Rosalyn. Was she disappointed? Yes. But she'd been raised to believe that everything happens for a purpose. Somewhere God was doing something that she couldn't yet see. What was it?

Rosalyn and her mom and dad were looking at all the alternatives when out of nowhere came an opportunity to be a semester missionary in Beirut, Lebanon. After they discussed the option, prayed about it, weighed the alternatives, and sought how this would fit in with God's ultimate mission for Rosalyn, she decided this was the right choice.

That semester in Beirut turned out to be a significant step in her journey toward fulfilling God's mission for her as well as growing her faith and dependence on Him. Rosalyn believed that not only had He called her but, having done so, He would meet her every need.

And guess what? While she was in Beirut, she was accepted to the University of Georgia and was able to return home at the end of the semester and fulfill her next step.

And here's what else was happening. While she was in Beirut, God was forging her with a wealth of experiences that strengthened her not only as she continued college but as she sought the life mission He'd planned for her . . . even before she was born.

A Picture Is Worth a Thousand Words

One of the hardest challenges we face as parents is illustrating the importance of key biblical principles for our kids. While most adults easily grasp abstract principles, kids, especially the younger ones, think in concrete terms. And studies show that in the postmodern culture of our society, stories and pictures are one of the most effective ways of conveying messages. So we offer two ideas: one for young kids and another for older ones.

If yours are younger, say, ages seven to fourteen, take them to a park with multiple paths or trails. Briefly show the kids a map of the park, and then put the map away—maybe in the car or your hip pocket. Tell the kids they're in charge of getting you to the chosen destination, but they can't refer back to the map. All they can do is try to remember the right twists and turns and choices at each crossroad.

Let them take the lead, and just watch what happens. Then go back and do it with a map and watch the amazing difference it makes.

Talk to them about how God gave His Word as a "map" for the choices we make in life. And the more we make our choices based on the truth of His Word, the more direct our paths will be in fulfilling the mission He's prepared for each of us.

If your kids are fifteen or older, find an opportunity, such as over a casual lunch or dinner, to talk about traveling. Ask how they would get from where you live to a well-known destination across the country, or to a location in your city that's a considerable distance from home. Challenge them to describe what streets or highways they would use (without looking at a map), including changes of routes at crossroads. And, no, they can't excuse themselves to check MapQuest! Unless your kids can memorize maps, they'll probably have difficulty describing a direct route from your home to the agreed-upon destination.

Then open a map and let them mark with a highlighter which route they would take and why.

These are opportunities to point out how God's "map" makes all the difference in directing us to the missions He has for our lives. Making a trip with the map in hand ensures we don't get lost, make wrong turns, or waste time and effort. That's an amazing picture of why God gave us His directions for making choices at the crossroads of life.[4]

Finally, be sure to tell your kids stories about times you faced the crossroads of choice. Share with them the joy and the triumph of making right, biblically based decisions, but when appropriate, admit to them that all your choices haven't been perfect. Let them know you're human. It's amazing what happens when a child sees a mom or dad willing to be vulnerable. Nonperfect people have more credibility—even to a child—and so the trust level goes up. It's worth the risk!

CHAPTER 21

MEET RHONDA AND RANDY SINGER

Remember the young woman from the last chapter who trusted God so completely with her future when she came to a crossroads of choice? She left her college in California, certain that God intended for her to enter the University of Georgia, which was close to her family. Yet she wasn't accepted, despite excellent grades and other prerequisites. But did she become angry or discouraged? No. She let God lead her at that crossroads, and as it turned out, He had a wonderful opportunity of a lifetime for her to serve as a semester missionary in Lebanon. Then, while she faithfully followed His plan, He arranged for her original hopes and desires to come true.

Do you wonder what kind of upbringing she had?

It was special, we assure you. Her parents are among the many who contributed their insights to this book, informing and inspiring our thinking as we researched and wrote. They are Rhonda and

Randy Singer, parents of Rosalyn. Their professional backgrounds
are teaching and coaching. Randy then fulfilled his dream of becoming a lawyer (and even an award-winning author of legal thrillers),
and Rhonda continues teaching, fully as dedicated to the minds and
hearts of other people's kids as she is to Rosalyn and her brother,
Joshua. In this chapter, we share some of their thinking.

Randy says one of the greatest responsibilities of parents is to
raise the next generation of missionaries.

> That happens in the home. It's not the responsibility of the church
> or the school. The first step is to develop an *on mission* mind-set
> in your children. Impress on them that they won't be in the per-
> fect will of God until they discover and participate in their role in
> the Great Commission.
>
> As parents, Rhonda and I believe that part of our Great
> Commission mandate is to be willing to put our children on the
> front line to do missions work. Sometimes that can be harder than
> going ourselves. But we don't want them to miss out on the great-
> est joy of life, which is the opportunity to see someone else come
> to Christ.

With that attitude and their faith in God's plan, we can see why
the Singers were able to hug their kids good-bye for mission work to
places such as Lebanon and Kenya for Rosalyn and Puerto Rico for
Josh. They don't believe, however, that you must cross an ocean to be
on mission; in fact, they know you don't even have to leave your zip
code, and this is a value they've been teaching their children by
instruction and example since they were toddlers. Says Randy:

> When our kids were young, we started taking them on our own
> mission experiences, allowing them to see us witnessing to people.
> We also talked around the kitchen table about *on mission* oppor-
> tunities we had experienced, allowing the kids to overhear our

conversations with each other about what happened. Let's say I shared Christ with someone while I was on a business trip. Of course, I wanted to tell Rhonda about it, so we could rejoice together, but I made a point to tell her in front of the kids. It's not as if you're bragging—you're just saying, "I had a chance to witness to this guy, and here's how it happened." What you're trying to do is model the behavior, show them how natural it is to talk about your faith in the normal warp and woof of life. What you want is for your kids to catch it, rather than feel as if you're teaching it to them.

Perfect Parents?

So the Singers model perfection, right? Hardly. Randy and Rhonda's kids have watched their parents fumble many witnessing opportunities. And he's famous for telling a story on himself about a time he filled the pulpit at his parents' church. Now a successful lawyer and sought-after speaker, Randy began his message to the congregation: "I know most of you came out tonight to see whether or not I'm still grounded. I'm just an example of how the grace of God can change anybody." Although, like others we interviewed, Randy doesn't believe it's necessary to detail his list of youthful mistakes, he acknowledges to Rosalyn and Josh that he made his share.

He credits his parents for handling him in a way that corrected him and motivated him to follow Christ:

They never disciplined me out of anger. They sat me down and laid it all out in logical fashion, especially when I was a teenager: "Here's what you did. Here are the consequences. Here's what's going to change in the next several months." Then they showed me the kind of grace, in terms of my spiritual walk, that God shows us. In other words, because my actions were sometimes contrary to what they believed—and even what I believed—they could have been judgmental, but they were accepting of where I was spiritually, yet committed to helping me become closer to Christ and more like Him.

Randy says his early years as a father amounted to "parenting by trial and error, fumbling around without any real strategy or intentionality." When he began to grasp the *on mission* concept for himself, he realized the importance of building it deliberately into his parenting. It was a process.

We'll close with more of his wisdom and ideas:

- When parents establish a strategy, how do they know it's working? First, look for whether you've seen or heard your children telling others about Christ, in their own way or words. If several months pass and they haven't had any experiences like that, then it's probably time for a course correction: an honest talk with them about the challenges and hurdles and holdups that keep them from doing it.

  Second, are your children comfortable building relationships with unsaved kids, or do they just hang with youth group members and Christian friends who think the way they do?

  Third, at some point you want them to take the initiative and suggest spiritual things they can do on their own: mission trips to take, camps for studying the Bible and honing their evangelistic skills, opportunities they want to take to invite unbelieving friends to church.

- As Rhonda and I saw the kids growing spiritually, we gave them more freedom—wings. In the spring of Rosalyn's junior year, we took a family vacation during spring break and told her, "As a young lady, you've earned our trust. From now on, these are the new rules you can live by." We did the same for Joshua.

- We encourage Rosalyn and Josh to do the family devotionals from time to time. It's good for everybody. The kids grow by preparing. We grow by learning from them instead of each other.

- We set aside funds beyond our tithe that allow us to send our kids on mission opportunities, so they don't have to raise money themselves. Not that we object to the practice—it's just our way of teaching that a big part of the *on mission* lifestyle is stewardship. It's also a way to free up the kids to solicit friends as prayer partners rather than sources of funding.

- When Rosalyn graduated from high school, I gave her a book I put together entitled *Who I Am*. Through photos, letters, poems, and story narrations, I reflected the *on mission* traits I was observing in her. It was a way to applaud Rosalyn for a job well done. I even included stories about her ancestors based on genealogy my father did.

  I wanted to show Rosalyn that she comes from people who were praying for her even generations before she was born. She's inherited not only their physical traits but also their spiritual legacy. So getting that book was part of her rite of celebration when she graduated from high school. It was a way to congratulate her and to demonstrate that it's time to step up, responsibility-wise, to say, "You're earning your wings."

CHAPTER 22

ONE STEP AT A TIME

PRINCIPLE 7

God guides you and provides for your mission one step at a time.

Key Scriptures

> I will instruct you and teach you in the way you should go;
> I will counsel you and watch over you. (Psalm 32:8)

> In his heart a man plans his course,
> but the LORD determines his steps. (Proverbs 16:9)

> Whether you turn to the right or to the left, your ears will hear a
> voice behind you, saying, "This is the way; walk in it." (Isaiah
> 30:21)

Trust in the LORD with all your heart
　　and lean not on your own understanding;
in all your ways acknowledge him,
　　and he will make your paths straight. (Proverbs 3:5–6)

Have we misled our children on the main message of Scripture? Have we wrongly communicated one of God's central expectations for our lives? Have we unintentionally caused some unfortunate consequences?

You may wonder, *What in the world are you talking about?* We're talking about the difference between victory and success, defeat and failure in the life of the Christian. And we're talking about how we as parents communicate this distinction to our kids. Too often, even well-meaning Christians suggest that God's ultimate goal for our lives is victory and success. But that message is backwards. The truth is that *God has promised victory and success as the inevitable result of our obedience.* What He wants most in the lives of our kids—and frankly, in the lives of us as parents—is obedience to His Word. That determines everything in life. But often we want to jump right to success, either bypassing or excusing the ultimate condition, which is obedience.

Jerry Bridges, author of *The Pursuit of Holiness,* affirmed this relationship: "God wants us to walk in *obedience*—not victory . . . Victory is a by-product of obedience."[1]

So What's the Big Deal?

What's the importance of this distinction? Let's examine how our obedience reflects what we really believe about authority figures in general—and God in particular. In daily life, people in positional authority sometimes force us to obey regardless of how we feel or what we believe. Think of a military officer giving orders to an enlisted soldier, a police officer redirecting traffic because of a road accident, or a principal establishing a new disciplinary rule affecting the whole school due to one disobedient student's actions. Their positions give them the power to enforce obedience in our lives. These are authorities we physically can see. They are imposing. They wear uniforms, or they occupy the corner office.

But God does not wear a badge. In fact, in the traditional sense, we don't see Him at all. He is not a dominating physical presence, and more to the point, He has called us to walk by faith. So the mandate of our obedience to Him is not so much *imposed on us* as it is *realized by us.* His instructions seem more subtle than the directions of the arm-waving cop rerouting traffic. (Yet the results of our disobedience to God's instruction often are not subtle!) And although that hardworking cop may be a nice guy, he really does not love us—and certainly not personally.

It's so important for us to convey these distinctions to our kids! Since God's mission for our lives is revealed in a progressive manner—step by step—the next step of our journey, and the clarity of which step to take, hinges on our obedience. We as parents must fully understand this, so we can effectively teach it to our kids.

Why is this concept so hard? We think it's because people generate some very unbiblical perceptions of God.

- Some see Him as a loving grandfather who, regardless of how we act or what our attitudes may be, will just smile indulgently, wink at our bad choices, and give us what we want anyway.

- Some see Him as a concierge. Whatever we want and need, all we have to do is tell Him our request and He hops to fulfill it—that's what He's there for, right?

- Others see Him as someone with whom we simply need to negotiate. "Come on, God, You know I'm not as bad

as Shane or Heather! So give me a break. If You'll do this
for me, I'll do something for You."

But God set the parameters in Isaiah 45 when He repeatedly
said, "I am the LORD, and there is no other." And if God is God,
then our primary responsibility as parents is to help our kids learn to
treat Him that way!

THE BIBLICAL BASE OF OBEDIENCE

As we help our kids grow and learn to fulfill God's plan for their
lives, we desperately need to help them understand the proper motivation for obedience to the One who created them. Without question, the ultimate basis is that *God is a God of love.*

Probably, most of our kids, if they can quote any Scripture at all,
can quote John 3:16. They even see it held up on banners at sport-
ing events. The central theme of that verse is God's love for us and
His willingness to do whatever it took to show that love—even the
sacrifice of His own Son on the cross.

The Old Testament repeatedly declares God's love for us. In
Jeremiah 31:3 God said, "I have loved you with an everlasting love;
/ I have drawn you with loving-kindness." There's no better way to
teach this concept than by following the instructions of Deuteronomy
6:6–7, where God counsels us as parents: "These commandments
that I give you today are to be upon your hearts. Impress them on
your children. Talk about them when you sit at home and when you
walk along the road, when you lie down and when you get up." We
as parents should work in the message of God's love as we talk to our
kids day in and day out, in the normal traffic patterns of life. Our
kids need to hear from us as their parents how we experience the loving hand of God in everyday events.

When something great happens in the life of your family, point
to the love of God. When some unexpected blessing comes, point to

the love of God. When someone attains an accomplishment, point to the love of God. And by all means, when God answers prayers, especially those in which the kids have been involved, point to the love of God. We have tried hard to do that at every turn, though we're sure we could have done a much better job.

But we want to share honestly with you that one of the greatest challenges we've struggled with as parents has been explaining incredibly difficult, even tragic, circumstances in our kids' lives. These have caused them to struggle deeply and honestly with the concept of the love of God.

In our own journey, we have probably experienced this most with our youngest. During her teens and in three consecutive years, Ashley lost three friends tragically to death—two in car accidents and one by suicide. The result? Regardless of how many times she'd heard about the love of God, she questioned that reality in view of those three tragic losses. Questions flooded her, such as

- If God is so loving, why did this happen?

- If God is all-powerful, why didn't He stop this?

- How does a God of love let such lousy and terrible things happen?

We share this honestly with you, because we want to make it very clear that "Sunday school answers" aren't enough. By that we mean that when the tough issues of life hit head-on, simplistic answers aren't going to be enough for our kids. They're going to wrestle with faith and trust. And they're going to question the very things they've been taught.

Here's what we did as a couple. First, you need to know that at about the same time Ashley's three young friends died, we also lost a dear pastor friend, Rick Ferguson. It seemed to us that he was far too young and vibrant to die, especially in the tragic way that he did, a car accident. So we told Ashley how much we were hurting. We let her see our pain, even to the point of admitting our natural human anger at and frustration with God for not preventing Rick's accident. We were open with her about our emotions, not only because we believe families should draw together at such times by being real and authentic, but because she needed the comfort of knowing we could relate. And then we reminded her that, *no matter what,* we know God is always in control. We quoted Isaiah 43:1–3, especially the middle verse:

> When you pass through the waters,
>   I will be with you;
> and when you pass through the rivers,
>   they will not sweep over you.
> When you walk through the fire,
>   you will not be burned;
>   the flames will not set you ablaze.

We reminded her that when emotions are this strong, we sometimes have to *choose* to believe in God's goodness, because circumstances don't seem to support what we were so sure of before we lost our beloved friend.

That's about as far as we could take her as parents, because as you know, we believe that children (as well as adults) must make a *personal* peace with God or it will not be authentic. We can *point* our kids to the truth of God's love, but we cannot *prove* it to them, especially when they're in a world of hurt. It's times like these that the rubber of our faith meets the road of life's reality.

DISCIPLINE, ACCOUNTABILITY, AND OBEDIENCE

But side by side with the love of God, we need to help our kids understand the justice of God. While He loves us and does not want to punish us, He is just and will discipline us for our sin. And He does this out of love, because we are His children: "My son, do not make light of the Lord's discipline, / and do not lose heart when he rebukes you, / because the Lord disciplines those he loves, / and he punishes everyone he accepts as a son" (Heb. 12:5–6).

It's here that the concept of accountability comes in. We are accountable to God for our actions and attitudes. But it's critically important to understand what the word *accountability* means in this context. It means answering to a Father who loves us, who wants the best for us, who has accepted us into His family and treats us as His sons and daughters.

Some people picture the term as meaning repression—God keeping His thumb on our lives so we don't have too much fun. How ridiculous that is biblically! In Bob's favorite painting of Jesus, He has His head thrown back and is engulfed in deep and resounding laughter. It's obvious that He's enjoying life to the fullest. And that's what He said He came to do, according to John 10:10: "The thief comes only to steal and kill and destroy; I have come that they may have life, and have it to the full."

It's critical to convey to our kids that we are accountable not to a tyrannical enforcer of law, but to One who wants us to become the very best we can be. Therefore, He wants us to live according to the principles and guidelines He has given us in His Word, because their purpose is to help us live life to the fullest.

One of the most important things we can do is help our kids discover that regardless of what we claim, we *are* what we do! We show obedience more in our actions than in our words.

God values obedience. We know this, because He uses the word so often in Scripture. He is constantly, throughout the Old and New Testament, calling His people to obey Him. And the reality is that *we do not discover God's unfolding will for the next step unless we have been obedient in the step we are presently taking.*

Scripture points out some key truths about the importance of obedience.

1. It's proof that we know God.

   We know that we have come to know him if we obey his commands. The man who says, "I know him," but does not do what he commands is a liar, and the truth is not in him. But if anyone obeys his word, God's love is truly made complete in him. This is how we know we are in him: Whoever claims to live in him must walk as Jesus did. (1 John 2:3–6)

2. It's proof that we love God.

   Whoever has my commands and obeys them, he is the one who loves me. He who loves me will be loved by my Father, and I too will love him and show myself to him . . . If anyone loves me, he will obey my teaching. My Father will love him, and we will come to him and make our home with him. (John 14:21, 23)

3. It's the way Jesus showed His love for God.

   For I have come down from heaven not to do my will but to do the will of him who sent me. (John 6:38)

4. It's the way we follow Christ's example.

   Whoever claims to live in him must walk as Jesus did. (1 John 2:6)

We have tried to teach our kids that regardless of what words come out of their mouths, if obedience to Christ is lacking, the words don't mean anything. We teach this on good authority due to the fact that Jesus Himself said, "Why do you call me, 'Lord, Lord,' and do not do what I say?" (Luke 6:46). Let's admit it: that's a question that begs to be answered.

We love what our friend Henry Blackaby says in his *Experiencing God* workbook concerning obedience:

In many ways, obedience is your moment of truth. What you DO will:

1. Reveal what you believe about Him.
2. Determine whether you will experience His mighty work in you and through you.
3. Determine whether you will come to know Him more intimately.[2]

ALLOW US TO SHINE SOME LIGHT ON THIS ISSUE

You know by now that we find it effective to show our kids what we mean by using picture language to flesh out principles found in God's Word. Illustration can make an abstract concept suddenly become concrete quicker than just about anything.

If you're trying to get this concept of God's guidance, one step at a time, into the lives of your kids, here's a neat way to do it. Get away from the city some evening, perhaps to a park or a state recreation area. If you like camping, that's a great place to do this. Wait until it's pitch-dark and you're away from human-manufactured lighting. Everything around you will be dark, and the stars above you will be bright. (A cloudy night works even better!) By then you'll be using a flashlight or some other kind of artificial illumination.

As you're moving along a path or walking down a road, warn your kids that you're going to turn out the light for just a moment because you want them to see how bright the stars are and how dark it really gets when you're away from the city. (Or if it's cloudy, you want them to experience total darkness.)

Then turn out the lights. As you know, it's weird when you can hardly see your hand in front of your face!

When everybody's ready, turn the light back on. Then point out how light is made to penetrate darkness. It's also created to help you see where you're going.

Then shine the flashlight right around where you and the kids are standing, and ask how far ahead they can see. Obviously, they can see only to the extent that the light reaches into the darkness.

Then ask how they would get to a place far beyond where the light ends. Obviously, the only way to do that is by moving forward so that the light itself moves ahead. In other words, you step into the light you already have, allowing the light you are holding to move forward to illuminate the darkness in which you cannot yet see. Explain that the flashlight you're holding is like the truth you've learned from your previous instruction from God. It illuminates the distance straight ahead, but now, to advance, you must take another step . . . and then another . . . and then another. Each step is illuminated by the light, or truth, of your previous instruction. And so you walk with Him.

You could do the same exercise at night in an unlit parking lot somewhere away from the city—perhaps a church parking lot that's located outside the suburban sprawl. Try to find a place where lights aren't everywhere. Bob's dad illustrated this to him on an old country road where they had a farm. Turn out the lights in the car for a minute and notice how far you can see. (Be sure the car isn't moving!) Then turn the lights back on, and discuss the same principles.

And a great truth that brings it all together is Psalm 119:105, "Your word is a lamp to my feet / and a light for my path."

Remember: If God is to guide us step by step as we discover and live out the missions He has for us, then we must be fulfilling the condition upon which the progressive revelation of His will for our life is based: our obedience to Him.

CHAPTER 23

MEET DIANE AND JAY STRACK

Few, if any, find the walk with God smooth. Yet the Stracks illustrate how God lays out an intricate path of steppingstones, guiding us and providing for our missions one step at a time.

Their backgrounds influenced their parenting. And they don't mind passing along their wisdom, because as Jay puts it, "We believe this stuff is caught as much as it's taught." He's talking about the *on mission* lifestyle, which he says his kids learn most effectively by seeing how he and Diane behave. But he's also talking about the parenting process itself, which he contends must be based on authenticity. "We figured out early on that not being authentic and genuine and consistent were the unpardonable sins in the eyes of the child."

Jay and Diane had contrasting upbringings, to say the least. She grew up in a big Italian family with a lot of love and security and displays of affection. But as she puts it, "there was no real spiritual direction in the home and no real direction for my life." She was determined to raise her kids with more intentionality.

POSTER BOY

Well, Diane hooked up with Jay, who could be the poster boy for growing up dysfunctional. We'll let him tell the story:

I came from six broken homes, a lot of physical, emotional, and sexual abuse. A lot of name-calling, yelling, screaming, alcohol, a brother given away and strangers in and out of our home. I didn't have the love or security Diane had. And I was clueless about what a father was supposed to be. I'd never really had one. I'd had a few bad ones, but they were never there very long. I'm living proof of what happens when you grow up in six homes, all broken because of alcohol. I became a teenage alcoholic myself and was busted for drugs four times.

So when Diane and I got together, we established guidelines. If we wanted our children to be kind, then we were going to have to be kind to one other. And we'd have to be very loving and kind to them. We would make a strong stand. If we wanted our children to say "No, thanks" to alcohol or drugs, then we couldn't disqualify ourselves by using alcohol, drugs, or tobacco.

We were resolute in our belief that as a married couple and as parents, we were going to follow Christ. To do that, we would model the kind of behavior we expected of them, because we wanted our children to be able to look at us. So we adopted a policy that our girls can watch whatever they see us watch. They won't get punished if they use language they've heard us use. They can go to whatever Web site we go to. They can take on whatever habits we have. The child's got to be able to reason, *I don't understand this rule,* or *I may not like this requirement, but Mom and Dad live by the same standards.*

What about telling their kids about past mistakes or family circumstances? Jay believes, "You've got to let them know what you've struggled with, but I don't think you need to go into the details." He wouldn't say, for example, "When I was fifteen, I was with this girl, and . . ." But Jay wants his girls to know the types of struggles he experienced.

I need to be able to say, "Honey, you got that from me, and that's a weakness and the Lord really had to give me strength for it." I've already told them, "If you ever feel an urge to take a drink or try a drug, I just want you to let Daddy know. If anybody on the planet will understand that urge, it will be me." You've got to be candid and straight with your kids. They have to know you can identify with them and steer them the right way.

TRAVELING HERO

An evangelist, Jay was on the road a lot during the early years. Traveling fathers (and mothers) are a fact of life today. But Diane handled it in a way that kept the family together and focused on Dad as the leader. Recalls Jay:

Diane, in my humble but accurate opinion, was the master at this, and I'll be forever grateful to her for making Dad out to be the hero. It was never "Dad's gone again," or "I can't believe Dad's not here," or "Ask your dad when he finally gets home." Those are negative messages, but there was never any of that. And it was hard on her. There are times when you're lonely or you hear things go bump in the night. Plus a lot of decisions come up where you suddenly have to be the strong one and stand in the gap.

Fortunately for our family, this remarkable lady made it out that when Dad came home, he was the hero. I bet the girls were ten or eleven before they stopped making signs for me that said "Welcome Home, Dad." Or they met me at the airport with hugs and kisses. Or they left me a note: "Wake me when you get home, so I know you're safe and sound."

Jay made his traveling years easier by calling the girls at the same time every afternoon when they got home from school and always calling in the evening to pray with them before they went to bed. He and Diane knew that kids need security from their earthly fathers as well as their heavenly Father.

CONSEQUENCES

How does a father with a checkered past—even if he *is* an evangelist—make certain his youthful exploits don't sound glamorous? A touchy question that we'll let Jay answer in his own words:

> At revivals I always made sure my girls were with me during decision time. I wanted them to see the tears. I wanted them to hear a young girl crying and wailing because of the bad choices she'd made. I wanted them to see the kid who was shaking visibly because of drugs. Or the one who snuck out of her parents' house and went to a nightclub and was given a date-rape drug.
>
> Same thing at our house: they saw all kinds of horrors that were tough to witness but definitely [created] teachable moments. I don't recommend these situations for every family, but this is the road I traveled, so it was a part of their family life. For example, my daughters were on the scene when we were trying to help someone who'd just thrown up in our living room while he was going through drug withdrawal.
>
> The only reason I talk about this stuff is to give kids hope. So many young people who come to hear me speak think that because of what they've been through, there's no hope for them. I want them to know about the hope of the Lord.
>
> But I [also] want my daughters to know about the conse-

quences of people's mistakes. So I often take them along and let them see a side of life that others don't see. They go with me to speaking engagements at colleges, to professional sports teams, and so on. For example, I'd done quite a few chapels for the Dallas Mavericks basketball team. A famous player named Roy was popular with my girls. They asked me, "Daddy, why don't they put in Roy?" And I'd have to answer, "Well, honey, Roy can't play anymore. Roy's gone back on drugs. The problem with drugs is they don't let go of you, and not everyone can walk away from them." So they learned there are consequences.

ROLE-MODELING

Diane was involved with a crisis pregnancy center, and their daughter Christina went to work there as a volunteer when she was only thirteen. She folded clothes or answered the phone. It was not uncommon for a woman who was pregnant to have several children with her. Maybe she was considering an abortion but was comparing her options by visiting the CPC. So Christina sometimes baby-sat the children while the mom received counseling.

One day, when Christina was fourteen and all the counselors were tied up with clients, a young woman became hysterical. Jay tells the story:

Chris came out of the storage room and began to counsel her. She'd heard the older women counseling, and she'd seen all the videos. In fact, she'd been through Evangelism Explosion training. So Chris showed this young woman the video about when life begins. And she wound up leading this twenty-three-year-old pregnant woman to the Lord.

The woman went on to have the baby and came in with her new bundle of joy to show Chris. So there was my daughter looking at a baby whose life had been spared and being told, "Because of you, I had this baby. Because of you, I made a wise choice."

This was an example of letting our daughter see reality up close and personal at a very young age. And she rose to the occasion. By the way, Chris recently received her master's degree in crisis and addiction counseling.

We'll close with more wisdom from Jay:

- The celebrity scene looks good, even to parents. But it's dangerous, the way celebrities dress, the way they act, the attention they get. Parents need to admit that. The way we practically worship celebrity is not harmless. Parents have to help their kids see beyond the glitter.

- I see too many parents trying to treat all their kids the same way. You have to be fair with each, but not recognizing their differences is a mistake. Our daughter Melissa had a hearing impairment, then seizures, and had to have open-heart surgery and corrective eye surgery. We learned that the greatest thing we could do was to give her structure because of her special needs: "Melissa, this is where your shoes are kept. This is when you do your homework. These are your chores. This is where your dog stays." She needed to be in bed at a certain time.

  Once she reached school age, Diane and I both felt what had to be our priority was giving Melissa structure. Yet *both* girls received our attention, just in different ways. Melissa had challenges and struggles that Christina never had. On the other hand, Christina had issues and opportunities that Melissa never had. So I believe you have to deal with each child. Train up a child in the way she should go—not that everybody's going to go in the same direction. But God knew that when He gave our children to us.

CHAPTER 24

WALKING WITH THE MAN

PRINCIPLE 8

When you answer God's call, you will experience His pleasure and change your world.

Key Scriptures

> We make it our goal to please him, whether we are at home in the body or away from it. (2 Corinthians 5:9)

> We speak as men approved by God to be entrusted with the gospel. We are not trying to please men but God, who tests our hearts. (1 Thessalonians 2:4)

> Whatever you do, work at it with all your heart, as working for the Lord, not for men. (Colossians 3:23)

Washed-out, weak, and wasted: that describes too many illustrations we've seen of Jesus! But let us tell you about our favorite painting of all time of the Master (which we mentioned earlier). The painting captures Him as a man's man with a rough beard, tan and strong with His head reared back in a laugh that obviously radiates all the way from His belly. In His eye is a sparkle showing His love of life and commitment to live it to the hilt. We loved that painting while we had it, and then somebody made off with it in the midst of one of our moves, and we've never found one like it since. We consider it one of our most significant losses, because it depicted Christ the way we picture Him in our hearts and minds.

So you can understand why we were so drawn to our friends Chuck and Jeanine Allen, who last fall sat in their darkened garage with a fourteen-inch TV plugged into their Jeep's lighter watching Donald Trump's *The Apprentice*. Obviously you're wondering why on earth they would choose such a strange place to share a family moment around one of TV's hottest shows. They laughed, provided running commentary, and exchanged opinions on who would hear the fatal words, "You're fired!" Well, rather than miss one of their favorite family activities in the midst of a power outage caused by a ferocious storm, Chuck and Jeanine decided that they could turn this "challenge" into a memorable family moment.

It's all the more amazing when you know the rest of the story. Chuck is an officer of the organization that Bob serves as president. Seven years ago, on the night of Bob's inauguration, Chuck called on his cell phone to share that Jeanine had been diagnosed with breast cancer. Their daughters, Amy and Amelia, were seven and nine at the time. Only two months earlier, Jeanine's mom had been diagnosed with pancreatic cancer, and she died eight months later. Also, Amelia's favorite teacher had died the previous spring from pancreatic cancer. Now the tragedy of cancer was striking even closer to home.

For seven years, we've watched Jeanine, Chuck, and their daughters valiantly and bravely fight the dreaded monster called *cancer*. The journey has been an emotional roller coaster with its mountains of hope and valleys of despair. The surgeries have been numerous, the radiation and chemo treatments unending.

But an amazing thing has continued to characterize the Allen household: it's the gift of joy and humor.

A Joyous Home

This is very important to us. It tracks with what we've learned in our study and research for this book on how to build an *on mission* mind-set into the lives of our kids. We've found one key ingredient in the homes of healthy, balanced, and committed Christian kids who seek God's plan for their lives and wind up wanting to change their world. That ingredient is simply this: a joyous home.

Chuck shares:

> When Jeanine and I married, we made a few decisions on the front end of our journey and have been committed to living with them ever since. We knew we wanted to have a joyous home, one filled with laughter and fun. We decided it was okay to kid one another and, in a healthy way, even to make fun of one other. We realized that if we were willing to laugh at ourselves and each other, we'd never run short of good material. And we were committed to not taking ourselves too seriously, while seriously enjoying one another.

Hardly anything is too sacred in the Allen home to be excluded as a potential point of humor. Take, for example, the first time Jeanine was losing her hair due to chemotherapy. One night she and the girls began to laugh and kid about the situation. Before long the girls were literally joining Jeanine in pulling clumps of hair out of her head and laughing riotously as it occurred. "You just had to be there to get it," says Chuck. "But we were committed to finding joy and fun even in the midst of life's most significant hurts. And Jeanine has been amazing in our family to help us stay on track."

It's in that home with such joy, in the midst of such difficulty, that Chuck and Jeanine have looked for teachable moments to share the importance of an *on mission* mind-set with their girls. We've mentioned that while some families sit down together with a devotional and prayer time, it's not easy for every family to do so, as Chuck relates.

> With our schedules as weird as they are, we decided early on to try to have a real significant family devotion time. In our minds, we'd all come together and go through books and all that kind of stuff. The problem was my two kids are so different that it just didn't fly. One's a reader, and one's not. One's highly athletic, and the other's highly social. The concept of a focused time of teaching spiritual truths just failed miserably at our home. So our question became: *how do we recognize family moments as learning opportunities, highlighting the principles of God?*

Boy, were we glad to hear that! That's exactly how it's worked in our family. While we wished that everybody would sit quietly and orderly for daily family devotions, it never seemed to work that neatly in our home. With three kids evenly spaced four years apart, our house was more like Grand Central Station than a quiet cathedral. Silence was never golden—in fact, it was hardly ever present!

Chuck regularly travels, and when he does, he seeks opportunities to share with people he meets the difference Christ has made in his life. And when it happens, he takes time around the dinner table to share his experience.

As for Jeanine, shortly after she was diagnosed with cancer, she asked Chuck to stop going to chemo treatments with her. Not because they were easy and she didn't need him, but because, as she put it, "A well person puts a crimp in the atmosphere. As all of us are sitting in chemo chairs, having a well person around stifles conversation . . . I can't share my faith in Christ as freely or effectively as when it's just we who are sick." And share she has: Jeanine has introduced several people in similar circumstances to the Christ who has changed her life.

When she comes home with exuberance, even in the midst of pain, she shares the triumph with her family and how she's experiencing God's pleasure through her obedience, even during the tough stuff.

AND IT'S WORKING . . .

Apparently, what Mom and Dad are sharing is working. Recently Amy, sixteen, wanted to take some friends to a church-related event. But Chuck was exhausted. He was helping take care of the house to alleviate some of Jeanine's pressure, holding down a full-time job (and then some), getting the kids where they needed to be at the right times and at the right places, and continually working on his own leadership and teaching skills. That night he hit a temporary emotional wall. "Amy, please, you're a cheerleader, you're doing everything in the world, now you want to go to an extra event— you're killin' me!"

Thoughtfully, Amy looked at him and responded: "But, Dad, they've encouraged us to bring kids who don't know Christ, and I was just trying to do what I see you and Mom doing all the time." She'd found two girls with shallow spiritual moorings, built a relationship with them, and invited them to the event. What she lacked was a ride. Chuck shared his thought processes with us:

All of a sudden I thought, *Oh, man, now my kid's spiritual, and I've got to do all this stuff I don't feel like doing! But I've got to give support to what I told her is important, what Jeanine and I have been*

*trying to model for her. I must be an idiot! What am I complaining
about? She's doing exactly what we've prayed she would do.*

You can imagine how Chuck felt when Amy came home on
Wednesday night sharing that the two kids had given their lives to
Christ. Crying and excited, Amy had indeed felt God's pleasure,
because she was doing exactly what Christ had come to do. In Luke
19:10, Jesus said that His whole purpose in coming was "to seek and
save those . . . who are lost" (NLT). And the pleasure Amy had seen
in Mom and Dad, in the midst of both good times and tough times,
was then hers to experience, even enjoy.

Chuck and Jeanine realize that both of their girls are very special, yet very different from each other. Amelia is the focused, hard-
driving, tenacious athlete. Amy is easygoing and steady, driven by
relationships—she never really meets a stranger. Seeing that the girls
are wired differently, Chuck and Jeanine have challenged each accordingly: Amelia using her athletic skills and participation as a bridge
over which to carry Christ to those with whom she plays and com-
petes; Amy using her relational skills to build rapport and friendships
through which Christ can become known to those in her circle of
influence. Both are increasingly experiencing God's pleasure as they
fulfill His calling in their lives, even while enjoying their different
personalities.

We Get to Do Something with God

Chuck and Jeanine are convinced of a key principle that leads to
experiencing God's pleasure: it's not that we've *got* to do something
for God; the truth is that we *get* to do something *with* God.

As Chuck puts it:

Sometimes we come across as if we've *got* to do this and we've *got* to
do that in order to be good, faithful Christians. Have you ever found

yourself saying, "I've got to go to church this morning," or "I've got to take the kids to their youth group meeting tonight"? Instead, we need to realize that we *get* to do this, and we *get* to do it in partnership with *God*. That change of focus can make all the difference.

It's amazing what we've learned as we've watched these friends traverse through such deep waters. Chuck told us about overhearing Jeanine talk on the phone with someone who also was struggling with cancer. He quickly gathered the girls out of Jeanine's line of sight and allowed them to listen to her speaking not from perceived strength, but from recognized physical weakness. Repeatedly she brought the caller back to the reality that Christ can be trusted—*no matter what!* "It's not your job to understand. Trust Him. You'll never understand cancer, and neither will the doctors. But for whatever reason, God has allowed you to have this. Find out what the reason is, what He wants to do in you—and through you—and then do it!"

As Chuck said,

When my girls hear their mother sharing like that, it may not be a formal family altar or an organized devotion. But it's their mom expressing how faithful God is, how much He loves her, and how much she has decided to trust Him. They will remember overhearing this conversation all their lives, especially when they are on their own, changing their world.

We simply said in our home: from the rising of the sun to the setting of the same, we're going to find the things of God, and we're going to enjoy them. We're going to feel His pleasure as we change our world.

The living testimony that our friends so openly shared says it all. It's a great reminder to us that whatever we're going through, whether good times or tough times, we can still experience God's pleasure and change our world . . . *right where we are!*

CHAPTER 25

MEET LINDA AND MIKE EBERT

You've met the Ebert family elsewhere in this book. They're the party animals who like to throw two huge get-togethers at Christmas: a "Happy Birthday, Jesus" party for kids and an *It's a Wonderful Life* party for adults. Besides the pure enjoyment of these parties, Linda and Mike use them as effective evangelistic outreaches to their neighbors—ways to get people together to begin relationships they hope and pray will lead to sharing Christ. Preparations for the parties are also good ways to involve their four children in creative, God-centered activities.

We can't think of a couple who does a better job of putting flesh on the principle: *when you answer God's call, you will experience His pleasure and change your world.*

The Eberts have sunny personalities and a positive outlook on life. Linda recalls taking their oldest to the Garden of the Gods in

Colorado Springs when they worked for Focus on the Family (Mike is now director of public affairs and special projects at the North American Mission Board). "Brandon was just a toddler. We looked at the scenery, and I said, 'Wow, look what God made for us to enjoy. I bet God knows you want to climb those rocks.' We were always bringing God into the equation. We pointed out that He provides things for us to learn from, to enjoy, to make us happy."

LEGACIES OF MISSIONS

Linda and Mike grew up seeing their parents integrate biblical principles into everyday life. "If we were watching a television show that Mom knew didn't honor God, she would turn off the TV," says Linda. "If we noticed some behavior in a public place that she knew didn't please God, we would discuss it as a family." Today she and Mike are proponents of making the most of opportunities on a daily basis to talk about godly values with the kids.

Their parents were missions-active people and set a good example. Linda's mother volunteered at crisis pregnancy centers. Linda remembers going with her one time to a young woman's apartment. "It was a total mess—not only messy but dirty. She was having a baby and needed someone to come alongside her with practical household help. So we did that." Another time Linda's mother befriended a couple from China.

ViYing and GiTu came to America, found that the job she had come for was denying them health benefits, and then learned she was pregnant. They decided to go to an abortion clinic. But someone intervened and told them they had options, directing them to the crisis pregnancy center where Mom worked. She was the one who met with them.

At Mom's funeral a couple of years ago, that Chinese couple came to pay their respects. With them came their son, who wouldn't have been born if she hadn't told them about Christ and helped them with the decision to keep their baby. We still get Christmas cards from that family. They are so caring and respectful because of Mom's legacy. We had wonderful role models.

Mike's parents came to know Christ while they lived overseas during a stint in the U.S. Navy. Says Mike:

While stationed in Japan during Vietnam, my dad was invited by a friend in the military to attend church. My folks had each attended mainline churches growing up, but they weren't going to church at that time. It happened to be a Southern Baptist church mission started by a missionary from the denomination. After a few weeks of attending, my dad prayed to receive Christ. And a couple of months later, my mom did as well.

Now they live near Mike and Linda in Georgia, where they relocated from Ohio. But they have the kind of retirement that continues to provide a model of ministry. Mike's parents have "adopted a family who isn't well off in many respects," explains Linda. "They've done everything they can to help out this family, such as taking the kids to vacation Bible school, even when the family doesn't want to 'do church.' We're glad our kids can see this *on mission* lifestyle in their grandparents."

In addition to throwing wonderful, God-honoring parties, here are more tips from Linda:

- Mike and I have been fortunate to live in several parts of the country. Wherever we've moved, we've sought role models, faithful couples who can mentor us with their parenting ideas. We need the challenge and motivation of people who have gone before us and will share their wisdom.

- When our kids need discipline, we bring up a Bible verse and ask them to write that verse twenty times on a sheet of paper. This is not to shove Scripture down their throats but to help put verses in their hearts that will guide them through life. So if something ugly comes out of their mouths, they might have to write Ephesians 4:29 on the paper: "Do not let any unwholesome talk come out of your mouths, but only what is helpful for building others up according to their needs, that it may benefit those who listen." And before they begin writing it, we talk about the principle that the verse teaches and how they're going to be amazed at how God's way of doing life is so much better than their own.

- We're always looking for ways to get to know our neighbors. We believe that forming a relationship must happen [before we share the gospel], and that takes time and effort. So maybe the kids and I will bake brownies and take them to a new family who's just moved in down the street. We'll say, "If there's anything you can't find while you're unpacking, just call us. We can bring it to you. Or if you need a fax machine, we have one at the house. You're always welcome to use it. And by the way, we have a church we'd love to recommend. If you're looking for one to visit until you know where you want to plant your feet, we'll be glad to take you to ours."

- The kids know about relationship building. Sometimes we'll be going through the neighborhood in our van distributing community newsletters. I'll shout to the kids, "Hey, everybody, why are we doing this?" They'll shout back, "To show them we care, so that one day we can tell them about Jesus!"

CHAPTER 26

NOW IT'S UP TO YOU, PARENTS AND GRANDPARENTS

Whathat do parents want most for their children? Is it really stuff—things? To be a step ahead of the Joneses? We don't think so.

In talking to parents in many parts of the world, we've found a common desire above all else: to see their children grow up and live successful adult lives, rooted in core values, prepared to make wise decisions with long-range positive impact, able to make contributions to the greater good, and with happy home lives of their own.

Parenting that results in this kind of success does not happen by accident, just as a space shuttle does not launch into the star-strewn sky and complete its mission by accident. Both endeavors take planning and intentionality. But unlike a spaceship engineered by man, we humans were put together by the greatest Engineer. And He built us for success. But He also put us into families, who can help guide us to the success He planned for us. That's where we as parents come in.

As we researched the wisdom and ideas of other parents we admire in preparation for this book, we were encouraged by those who have taken seriously their roles as Mission Control in the lives of their children. For example, do you remember the Pucketts? We introduced them to you in the beginning of the book as they celebrated their son's baptism with a party that could reach nonbelievers with the gospel, a process we call being *on mission*. That's when we live out our role in the Great Commission by deliberately building into our lives opportunities to share Christ with people who don't claim Him as Lord and Savior. It's when we live intentionally for God.

Well, we have another story about the Pucketts. It's a special way they mark a rite of passage for their kids: going off to college.

It started with their oldest, Puck. When they drove him to the college that would educate and prepare him for his life's occupation, they took along a small vial of oil. They knew that his life would change dramatically in the next four or so years, and they wanted to mark it with more than helping him move into the dorm.

When they got there, they gathered together to pray. Then, using a tiny bit of oil, they anointed his head and asked God to be in charge of his thoughts and help him to learn. They anointed his hands and asked God to teach him the right way to use them in honest, strong work. They anointed his feet and asked God to direct him along the right path and keep him there, safe in His direction, walking in His way.

A small vial of oil and a few minutes of prayer—but prayer with such purpose! Can you imagine how memorable was that moment, not only for the college freshman but for his whole family? What a launch into his future!

And do you remember reading about our friend Allan Taylor? We have another idea to share with you from his family's thoughtful way of giving wings to their children. The Taylor family has developed what they call the Taylor Code of Conduct:

1. Honor God and His Word.
   A Will to obey.
   This is Vision.

2. Respect the dignity of others.
   A Worthiness to give.
   This is Value.

3. Possess impeccable character.
   Wisdom to embrace.
   This is Virtue.

4. Protect the fidelity of a woman's purity.
   A Woman to love.
   This is Valor.

5. Reject passivity and accept responsibility.
   A Work to do.
   This is Victory.

We invite you to find and embrace your family's way of providing roots (like the Taylor Code of Conduct) in order to give the blessing of wings (like the Puckett anointing ceremony). These ideas work for these families. But they may be way off-base for yours. You must find your own. And what an adventure it will be!

So *it's up to you*, parents and grandparents. You are Mission Control and the ground crew. And your mission is to launch godly children. It's an impossible job to do alone. But with God's help, you can do it. And, remember, the sky really *is* the limit.

> To stay in touch with us and
> for new and fresh ideas,
> visit us at
> totallifeimpact.com.

Your Guide to Personal Commitment

God's Design

Abundant and Eternal Life for You!

God loves you. He wants you to enjoy all the peace and joy of an abundant and eternal life.

> The **BIBLE** says . . .
> "For God so loved the world that he gave his one and only Son, that whoever believes in him shall not perish but have *eternal life.*"—John 3:16, italics ours

> **JESUS** says . . .
> "I have come that they may have *life,* and have it to the full."—John 10:10, italics ours

It is unmistakably clear that *God wants* everyone *to experience the peace and joy of abundant and eternal life.*

Why then have most people missed this reality?

Your Dilemma

Separation from God

God created man in His own image. (See Genesis 1:27.)

Instead of making us mindless robots that automatically love and obey Him, God gave us an individual will and freedom of choice.

Man rebels against God and disregards His protective commands and instructions. The Bible calls this self-centered rebellion "sin."

Sin is failure to be what God wants you to be . . . and results in failure to do what God wants you to do.

> The **BIBLE** says . . .
> "Anyone, then, who knows the good he ought to do and doesn't do it, sins."—James 4:17

Every *person is guilty of this sin . . .*

> The **BIBLE** says . . .
> "All have sinned and fall short of the glory of God."—Romans 3:23

> "If we say that we have no sin, we deceive ourselves, and the truth is not in us."—I John 1:8 NKJV

This sin separates you from Holy God . . .

No matter how hard you try to be perfect, you cannot bridge the gulf that this sin brings between you and God.

God is offering you the only escape from sin's eternal penalty of separation from God . . .

GOD'S DELIVERANCE

THE CROSS
The only answer to your sin problem is the Lord Jesus Christ.

Jesus died on the cross and paid the penalty for your sin. His death and resurrection from the dead bridged the gulf separating you from God.

> The **BIBLE** says . . .
> "But God demonstrates his own love for us in this: While we were still sinners, Christ died for us."—Romans 5:8
>
> "For the wages of sin is death, but the gift of God is eternal life in Christ Jesus our Lord."—Romans 6:23

Jesus is not merely one of many ways to God's forgiveness and eternal life. Nor is Jesus simply the best way to God. God has made Him the *only* way to a loving personal relationship with Him.

JESUS HAS ALREADY PAID THE PRICE FOR YOU!

> The **BIBLE** says . . .
> "Salvation is found in no one else, for there is no other name under heaven given to men by which we must be saved."—Acts 4:12
>
> **JESUS** says . . .
> "I am the way and the truth and the life. No one comes to the Father except through me."—John 14:6

Jesus offers abundant and eternal life to all who will surrender their lives to the Lordship of Jesus Christ. You must make the choice . . .

YOUR DECISION

RECEIVE CHRIST
By personally inviting and receiving Christ to be your Lord and Savior, you can place your trust in Jesus Christ to save you today.

> **JESUS** says . . .
> "Here I am! I stand at the door and knock. If anyone hears my voice and opens the door, I will come in . . ."—Revelation 3:20

Admit your need. "I am a sinner in need of God's forgiveness."

Honestly *repent* (turn from) your sins. God does not desire that any man seek to change his own life by his own strength. *Only God can do this.* However, there can be no true saving faith without repentance.

Repentance is a godly sorrow about sin that will produce . . .
> a change of attitude about God and about sin.
> This will lead to . . . a change of direction in life.
> This will evidence itself in . . . a change of action.
> You will seek to please God.

> The **BIBLE** says . . .
> "Repent, then, and turn to God, so that your sins may be wiped out, that times of refreshing may come from the Lord."—Acts 3:19

Stop trusting yourself and your good work to qualify you for heaven. No one can "earn," "deserve," or "work" his or her way to heaven.

> The **BIBLE** says . . .
> "For it is by grace you have been saved, through faith—and this not from yourselves, it is the gift of God—not by works, so that no one can boast." —Ephesians 2:8–9

Commit Your Life to Christ

You must surrender control of your life to Jesus. He both *desires* and *deserves* to be Lord (or "Boss") of your life. Jesus will never be satisfied with "second place." You must be willing to make Him the most *important* person in your life.

> The **BIBLE** says . . .
> "If you confess with your mouth, 'Jesus is Lord,' and believe in your heart that God raised him from the dead, you will be saved. For it is with your heart that you believe and are justified, and it is with your mouth that you confess and are saved."—Romans 10:9–10

You can receive Christ right now by faith through prayer.

God knows your inner being and is not so concerned with your words as He is with the attitude of your heart. The following is a suggested prayer.

> "Lord Jesus, I realize I am a sinner. I am truly sorry for my sins. I know You died on the cross to pay for my sins. Right now, I turn from my sins and invite You into my heart. I give You control of my life to be my Lord. I trust You now to be my Savior. Change my life and help me to live for You in the fellowship of Your church. Amen."

Does this prayer express the desires of your heart? If it does, you can pray right now and **Christ will come into your life as He promised.**

Now, how would you answer these two questions?

Question 1:
> Have you come to the place in your spiritual life that you know for certain, if you died today, you'd go to heaven?

Question 2:
> Suppose you were to die today; standing before God, if He asked you, "Why should I allow you into heaven?" what would you say?

Where is Christ right now in relation to you according to Revelation 3:20?

"Here I am! I stand at the door and knock. If anyone hears my voice and opens the door, I will come in and eat with him, and he with me."

Your Assurance

Promises to You from God's Word

Eternal life is the unending, indivisible relationship between you and God, which begins the moment you receive His Son, Jesus Christ. God Himself promises it!

> The **BIBLE** says . . .
> "Yet to all who received him, to those who believed in his name, he gave the right to become children of God."—John 1:12

> **JESUS** says . . .
> "I tell you the truth, whoever hears my word and believes him who sent me has eternal life and will not be condemned; he has crossed over from death to life."—John 5:24

If you are trusting Jesus Christ *alone* for your salvation, what are you now promised as having?

> **JESUS** says . . .
> "Whoever believes in the Son has eternal life . . ."—John 3:36

According to God's own promises, who has eternal life?

> **JESUS** says . . .
> "My sheep listen to my voice; I know them and they follow me. I give them eternal life, and they shall never perish; no one can snatch them out of my hand."—John 10:27–28

Under what circumstances would Christ leave you?
According to this, how many times is it necessary to receive Christ?

> The **BIBLE** says . . .
> "And this is the testimony: God has given us eternal life, and this life is in his Son. He who has the Son has life; he who does not have the Son of God does not have life. I write these things to you who believe in the name of the Son of God so that you may know that you have eternal life." —1 John 5:11–13

According to the above verses . . .
> In whom is eternal life found?
> Who has eternal life?
> Do you have eternal life?
> When did eternal life begin for you?

God's promises and character cannot lie. They cannot be earned. You receive them the moment you place your faith in Christ Jesus.

Even though feelings are important, *your relationship with Christ is based on facts,* not on feelings that can change daily.

Notes

Chapter 5

1. Rolf Garborg, *The Family Blessing* (Tulsa: Harrison House, 2001), 21.

Chapter 6

1. Shaunti Feldhahn, *For Women Only* (Sisters, Ore.: Multnomah Press, 2004), 55.
2. Ibid., 65.

Chapter 7

1. James Dobson, *Parenting Isn't for Cowards* (Waco: Word Publishers, 1987), 210–11.
2. Gary Smalley and John Trent, *The Gift of Honor* (Nashville: Thomas Nelson, 1987), 109.
3. Rabbi Jeffrey K. Salkin, *Putting God on the Guest List* (Woodstock, Vt.: Jewish Lights Publishing, 1998), 17.

Chapter 10

1. The pamphlet *Your First Nine Months* (Wheaton, Ill.: Good News Publishers, 1991).
2. Ron Jenson, *Achieving Authentic Success* (San Diego: Future Achievement International, 2001), 98–99.
3. Used by permission of Dr. Mels Carbonell, Uniquely You Resources. For more information, call 706-492-5490 or go to *www.uniquelyyou.com*.

Chapter 14

1. Leonard Ravenhill, *Jonathan Edwards: Portrait of a Revival Preacher* (Minneapolis: Bethany House Publishers, 1963).
2. Richard Louis Dugdale, *The Jukes: A Study in Crime, Pauperism, Disease and Heredity* (New York: Putnam's Sons, 1877, and Arno Press, 1970).

Chapter 20

1. Beth Moore, *Believing God* (Nashville: Broadman & Holman, 2004), 5.
2. Ibid.
3. Henry Blackaby and Claude King, *Experiencing God* (Nashville: LifeWay Press, 1990), 113.
4. While these are activities we recommend, other activities can drive home Christian truths to your kids. Check out the Heritage Builders materials from Focus on the Family. Jim Weidmann and his team have done amazing work. Visit *www.heritagebuilders.com*.

Chapter 22

1. Jerry Bridges, *The Pursuit of Holiness* (Colorado Springs: NavPress, 1978), 21.
2. Blackaby and King, *Experiencing God,* 147.

About the Authors

Bob Reccord is president of the North American Mission Board and is the host of *Strength for Living* radio show. He is the author of *When Life Is in the Pits, Forged by Fire, Beneath the Surface,* and coauthor of *Made to Count* and *Live Your Passion, Tell Your Story, Change Your World.*

Cheryl Reccord has committed her life to raising three wonderful kids and equipping them for adulthood. She is a popular speaker and the author, with Linda Ebert, of *Freedom from Fear.* She also serves as president of Total Life Impact, an organization focused on helping people make their lives count through life coaching, training, and equipping.